Meridian Tapping And The 72 Holy Names Of God

Copyright information

Copyright © 2015 by Doron Alon

Alon, Doron

Meridian Tapping And The 72 Holy Names Of God
—1st ed

ISBN: 0-9824722-5-0

Printed in the United States of America

Cover image : 800px-Hebrew_Bible_Wordle_-_בתנ_המלים_התפלגות_פוסטר_ר' - Wikimedia - Dav!dB

Book Cover Design: Doron Alon

INTRODUCTION

Many Are The Names Of God And Infinite The Forms Through Which He May Be Approached - Ramakrishna

If you have read my other books in the "Tapping Miracles Series" you know that I try to provide new ways of applying Meridian Tapping. Meridian Tapping has been PROVEN to work, there is no doubt about that. We know that that are several ways Meridian Tapping can be used. We know that there are several ways to approach the life of spirit. Both Spirit and Meridian Tapping are based on universal principles that I think most, if not all of us agree is real and true. Since both Spirit and Meridian Tapping are so diverse, yet universal at the same time, I think it is more than appropriate to combine the Power of Spiritual Paths and Meridian Tapping. Meridian Tapping is like a universal key. It can unlock the potential in every single modality we introduce it to.

In this book, we will apply Meridian Tapping and The 72 Holy Names of God that has been gleaned through the Sanctified Paths of Jewish Mysticism known as the Kabbalah. Although This book is not specifically about the Kabbalah, it does have veins of the mystical tradition throughout it.

This book is a bit longer than the others in this series because we will be going through every single Name of God and doing a tapping session with each one . In the coming chapters I will, of course, explain what Meridian Tapping is. Then we will proceed to the 72 Names of God and How to incorporate them into a Meridian Tapping Practice.

Once you incorporate the Names into your practice a new world of possibilities can open up for you. The names themselves are hidden within the Bible. Within the text lies the keys to spiritual and material growth. Within the names of God resides the secrets of the cosmos. Within the bible hides the 72 names of God.

Chapter 1: Levels Of Inquiry

I grew up in an odd family. My mother's side is Irish Catholic and my father's side Jewish with Middle Eastern origins. We used to celebrate both Jewish and Christian holidays. I had an extra benefit, I was born on December 31, so I always lucked out. I would get presents for Hanukah, Christmas and my birthday all within 10 days of one another. I guess you could say I was spoiled rotten :) .

Although I was raised predominantly Jewish despite the mix. As I grew older, I eventually left the tribe so to speak. I realized that I was not happy boxing in my spirituality. My mind , heart and soul needed to experience spirit on so many levels. Until this day I always dive into the deep waters of spirituality. If you read my other books you can see that I essentially embrace all forms of the spiritual and deeply so.

This spiritual freedom that I found myself experiencing led me down many paths. One of them was Jewish mysticism also known as the Kabbalah. It helps that I can read Hebrew and some Aramaic so I can work with those texts a bit more. The Kabbalah for all intents and purposes is the mystical arm of Judaism. Its function is to delve deeply into the Old testament and glean hidden secrets within the text. **It is, in reality, much larger than any one religious tradition.**

There is a school of thought in Judaism that states that there are 4 levels of inquiry into the old testament.

> Level 1: Is the Surface and Literal meaning of the text itself.
> Level 2: Are hints of a deeper meaning beyond the surface text.
> Level 3: A Deeper Practical inquiry
> Level 4: The Secret and esoteric meaning behind the texts

Each of these levels stands alone, but do not contradict one another. In fact, if you do go up the levels you will find that the former level is included as well. I guess you can say that each level transcends the other, but includes it as well.

With this in mind, we will be focusing more on level 4. The reason for this is that the 72 Holy Names of God were gleaned via these secret methods. Before we go on to the 72 Holy Names of God, I'd like to get a few things out of the way. Lets jump in.

Chapter 2: So, What's In A Name?

Although names are essentially tools to allow us to distinguish one thing from another and one person from another person, they also carry deeper significance. In every religious traditions, the name has power and meaning. For Example, the name Jesus indicates his role in the world as a savior. Moses name indicates that he was " pulled up from the water".

In the Buddhist and Hindu traditions; The names of the Gods are used extensively through Mantras In ancient Egypt, there was heavy emphasis on knowing the "name" of an individual or of God. There is a legend in ancient Egyptian lore that states Isis Knew the real Name of the God Ra and that gave her the immense magical power she was known for.

In the Jewish Mystical tradition, the Name of God is the backbone of all existence. Books such as the Sepher Yezirah and Sefer Raziel are dedicated to the power of letters and names and how they were used to create the universe. Mystics have used the divine name and the letters of God's name to change events.

It is said in the Jewish tradition that if a person could decipher the true name of God, they would have the power to destroy the universe. In this book, we will harness the 72 holy names of God through Meridian Tapping. You will know Gods 72 names and thus be able to channel the power of those names to change your life. We will need to glean the names from the Hebrew original of the verses I will teach you in a future chapter.

Please note, you will not need to know Hebrew in order to use them in your meridian tapping session. All you will need is to gaze and utter the letters that will transliterated for you as you go through the tapping session. But before we delve into the names, let us understand why Hebrew is such an important language for tapping into the power of these 72 holy names of God.

Chapter 3: The Power of A Letter

The Hebrew alphabet , like Sanskrit is an energetic language, each letter is significant and in and of itself contains power when you utter them or think about them.

Even just looking at them can bestow power on you. This is very important to remember because you do not need to understand what they mean in order to gain power from them. Its like gravity, you see its pull on everything. But do you truly know how it came about exactly? We might know the very basics, but the math behind gravity is mind boggling and I am NOT a math person . :) All I know is that it exists. You see what I mean? The same goes for the 72 holy names of God you will read here.

The Hebrew Alphabet is comprised of 22 letters with 5 additional letters that are used at the end of words. In the Ancient and mystical text called the Sefer Yezirah (Book Of Creation), the Hebrew letters are the very foundation of all of creation. Please reference the chart below of the Hebrew letters. The letters are read from right to left.

Each letter has a meaning, but in the spirit of brevity ,I will not go into the meanings of each letter since it is not necessary for our purposes. These names as a whole create power and meaning that transcend the individual letters they are constructed of. I am just going to give you an overview as to why the Hebrew letters are so important for us.

As I mentioned earlier, the ancient Jewish mystical book called the Sefer Yezirah presented the power of the

Hebrew letters. The book itself is somewhat of a mystery and it is rather short. But my goodness is it complex. As legend would have it, supposedly this book was revealed to the patriarch Abraham. This means that from the earliest days of humanity, someone knew the secrets of the cosmos. Through the years many mystics have studied it and have used to successfully create miracles.   If you'd like a copy of the Sefer Yezirah, I recommend "Sefer Yetzirah: The Book Of Creation By Aryeh Kaplan."

The Hebrew alphabet looks rather simple when you look at it but that is the beauty. Within the letters, the deepest secrets of the cosmos resides.

When you simply gaze at them you are activating creative forces. The very same ones that created the universe. It is for this reason we will be using the 72 names of God in their original Hebrew font. Since the letters together create the energy force within the name.

As you can see, this was a brief overview as to why the Hebrew letters are so powerful . I could have gone on for several hundred pages about each one, but I figure you bought this book to transform your life NOW. If you would like to learn more about the Hebrew letters and their significance there is a great book called "The Wisdom In the Hebrew Alphabet".

In the next chapter we will go on a quick detour before going into the 72 names. In the next chapter, I will explain the Meridians and Meridian Tapping. If You have read my other books on this topic you can skip to Chapter 5.

Chapter 4: Meridians and Meridian Tapping

Meridian Points

There are many meridian points in the body. These points are located on the physical body as well as throughout the energetic system. They are used to transport energetic substances in and out of our bodies, both subtle and physical.

They are, in essence, channels for your life force. We have gleaned the various meridian points from Chinese acupuncture. Our quality of life depends on the ease of which energy flows throughout these points. In order to remain healthy in both mind and body, the meridian points must be cleared. Not unlike our bodies, any blockages in our energy can mean the difference between life and death. If there are any blockages, they can cause untold misery in your life, both physically and mentally. Since these points are throughout the body, any blockage in any of them inevitably causes physical ailments as well. The Meridians that are in the energy system are channels for our many thoughts and feelings both positive and negative. When the energy is blocked, we grow complacent with life. We isolate from others and can often fall into deep depression. These blocks also cause us to make decisions that we would not make if we were clear. I should know, I was one big energetic block. My life was in turmoil because of it ...So I speak from experience. I ate too much, weighed too much, drank too much and ruined a perfectly wonderful relationship. It's safe to say that my energy was chaotic and several blockages were present.

Since the meridians are conduits of energy, they are very important for the energy flows in and out of us. Since these Meridian points are vast in number, it's impossible to cover them in one book. We will cover the main ones.

Meridian Tapping AKA EFT:

Perhaps you have heard about EFT, it has been very popular for many years amongst the energy healing crowd. EFT is an acronym for Emotional Freedom Technique and as the name implies, it is a method of freeing yourself from negative emotional states. It alone is highly effective and the EFT methods are evolving every day and becoming even more effective. People have found relief and even cures for chronic painful conditions. EFT is one of the most effective modalities in existence.

EFT aka Meridian Tapping is a form of psychological acupressure that uses the traditional ancient Chinese acupuncture points that correspond to the meridians of the body. Instead of using needles however, you would use your fingers to gently tap on the various meridian points. As you tap you will also express the issue you are having, either out loud or in your mind. The combination of verbalization and tapping create a very powerful synergy. And it is even more powerful when using it with the 72 holy names of God.

EFT evolved over time from a technique called "Thought field therapy." T.F.T also includes tapping meridian points but was a bit more complex in its approach. Gary Craig, a performance coach from California eventually simplified the approach and called it EFT. He chose a set of meridian points to focus on and developed the technique around them. The wonderful thing about Meridian tapping is that it doesn't take a long time to implement. In less than 2 minutes you can go through an entire cycle of meridian points. For the purposes of this book, I am going to use some Gary Craig's choice of Meridian points since they are the least complicated and are easily accessible. As I mentioned earlier, Meridian tapping is a very powerful approach to releasing emotional blocks and various physical conditions that cause pain. When you tap meridian points it affects your entire energy system and that is why it often yields such dramatic results. It is also very powerful against addictions, depression, phobias. It can also be used to imprint positive goals on to your subconscious mind. In short, it is a technique that can transform your life. I will explain where these points are on the body. I tend to start with the top of my head and move down to the karate chop point, I find this mixes it up a bit and makes th energy flow betetr so that is how I itemized the tapping points. You may start at the karatae chop point and move up the points as you please. I find that the order really doesnt make a difference. I think people like the order because it seems eaiser, but it doesnt really matter which point you tap on first in my estiamtion.

Tapping points:

Top of Head

Eyebrow point: Right to the side of the bridge of the nose on either side.

Side of the eye: Right below the temple, either side is good.

Under eye:

Under the nose: Right above the mouth

Chin point: Located right under the lower lip

Collar bone: Around the sternum area.

Under arm point: Literally right under your arm pits.

Karate chop point: on either hand.

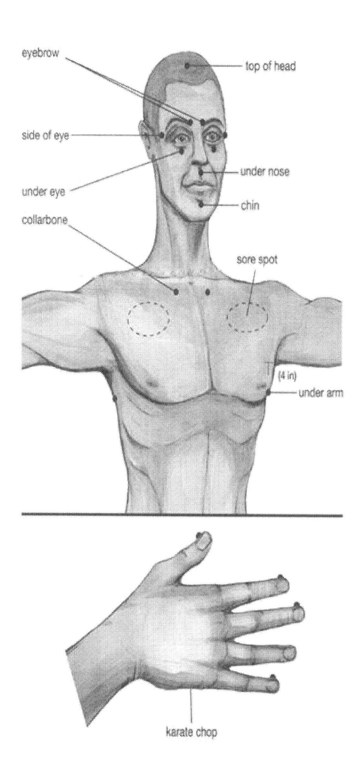

In the next chapter we will get deeper into the 72 names and how to use them.

Chapter 5: The Significance Of The 72 Names Of God

The 72 names of God is derived from the book of Exodus chapter 14 verses 19-21. In reality, the 72 Names of God are essentially 1 name comprised of 216 letters. So in that sense it is a name with 72 parts. The name is divided into triads which means that every name is comprised of 3 letters. To create the first name you combine the first letter of Verse 14:19 the last letter of Verse 14:20 and the first letter of verse 14:21. You would continue this until all the letters in these verses are used.

Here is the English translation of these verses:

" [19] Then the angel of God who was going before the host of Israel moved and went behind them, and the pillar of cloud moved from before them and stood behind them, [20] coming between the host of Egypt and the host of Israel. And there was the cloud and the darkness. And it lit up the night[a] without one coming near the other all night.

[21] Then Moses stretched out his hand over the sea, and the LORD drove the sea back by a strong east wind all night and made the sea dry land, and the waters were divided." - - Exodus 14:19-21

Here is what these verses look like in Hebrew.

יט וַיִּסַּע מַלְאַךְ הָאֱלֹהִים, הַהֹלֵךְ לִפְנֵי מַחֲנֵה יִשְׂרָאֵל, וַיֵּלֶךְ, מֵאַחֲרֵיהֶם; וַיִּסַּע עַמּוּד הֶעָנָן, מִפְּנֵיהֶם, וַיַּעֲמֹד, מֵאַחֲרֵיהֶם.

כ וַיָּבֹא בֵּין מַחֲנֵה מִצְרַיִם, וּבֵין מַחֲנֵה יִשְׂרָאֵל, וַיְהִי הֶעָנָן וְהַחֹשֶׁךְ, וַיָּאֶר אֶת-הַלָּיְלָה; וְלֹא-קָרַב זֶה אֶל-זֶה, כָּל-הַלָּיְלָה.

כא וַיֵּט מֹשֶׁה אֶת-יָדוֹ, עַל-הַיָּם, וַיּוֹלֶךְ יְהוָה אֶת-הַיָּם בְּרוּחַ קָדִים עַזָּה כָּל-הַלַּיְלָה, וַיָּשֶׂם אֶת-הַיָּם לֶחָרָבָה; וַיִּבָּקְעוּ, הַמָּיִם.

According to the Jewish Mystical tradition, the discovery of the 72 names was a huge spiritual breakthrough. The prime text in the Jewish mystical tradition (The Zohar) states that the moment Moses discovered the 72 names and how he could use them this changed everything for the Jewish people. As they were crossing the Red Sea at first, the water did not part. They were up to their necks in water. But when , In faith Moses used the 72 names of God, the water parted. In was only after this event did the actual verses get put on paper. As you can see, it is not so much history as it is a story behind the name and where it came from. This lack of historical evidence is by no means an indication that it is not true or powerful . As I stated in the introduction, there are 4 levels of biblical exegesis, the deriving of the 72 names is the fourth level.

For Illustrative purposes I will show you how some of the names are derived from the 3 Hebrew verses.

For the first name, I will highlight the letters in yellow, second name in red and third name is green. I will not go through this process for every name, I just want to show you how the names were derived. All the names will be extracted for you at the end of the chapter so you do not need to do this laborious process yourself.

Name one:

יט וַיִּסַּע מַלְאַךְ הָאֱלֹהִים, הַהֹלֵךְ לִפְנֵי מַחֲנֵה יִשְׂרָאֵל, וַיֵּלֶךְ, מֵאַחֲרֵיהֶם; וַיִּסַּע עַמּוּד הֶעָנָן, מִפְּנֵיהֶם, וַיַּעֲמֹד, מֵאַחֲרֵיהֶם.

כ וַיָּבֹא בֵּין מַחֲנֵה מִצְרַיִם, וּבֵין מַחֲנֵה יִשְׂרָאֵל, וַיְהִי הֶעָנָן וְהַחֹשֶׁךְ, וַיָּאֶר אֶת-הַלָּיְלָה; וְלֹא-קָרַב זֶה אֶל-זֶה, כָּל-הַלָּיְלָה.

כא וַיֵּט מֹשֶׁה אֶת-יָדוֹ, עַל-הַיָּם, וַיּוֹלֶךְ יְהוָה אֶת-הַיָּם בְּרוּחַ קָדִים עַזָּה כָּל-הַלַּיְלָה, וַיָּשֶׂם אֶת-הַיָּם לֶחָרָבָה; וַיִּבָּקְעוּ, הַמָּיִם.

Name two:

יט וַיִּסַּע מַלְאַךְ הָאֱלֹהִים, הַהֹלֵךְ לִפְנֵי מַחֲנֵה יִשְׂרָאֵל, וַיֵּלֶךְ, מֵאַחֲרֵיהֶם; וַיִּסַּע עַמּוּד הֶעָנָן, מִפְּנֵיהֶם, וַיַּעֲמֹד, מֵאַחֲרֵיהֶם.

כ וַיָּבֹא בֵּין מַחֲנֵה מִצְרַיִם, וּבֵין מַחֲנֵה יִשְׂרָאֵל, וַיְהִי הֶעָנָן וְהַחֹשֶׁךְ, וַיָּאֶר אֶת-הַלָּיְלָה; וְלֹא-קָרַב זֶה אֶל-זֶה, כָּל-הַלָּיְלָה.

כא וַיֵּט מֹשֶׁה אֶת-יָדוֹ, עַל-הַיָּם, וַיּוֹלֶךְ יְהוָה אֶת-הַיָּם בְּרוּחַ קָדִים עַזָּה כָּל-הַלַּיְלָה, וַיָּשֶׂם אֶת-הַיָּם לֶחָרָבָה; וַיִּבָּקְעוּ, הַמָּיִם.

Name Three:

סיט |

יט וַיִּסַּע מַלְאַךְ הָאֱלֹהִים, הַהֹלֵךְ לִפְנֵי מַחֲנֵה יִשְׂרָאֵל, וַיֵּלֶךְ, מֵאַחֲרֵיהֶם; וַיִּסַּע עַמּוּד הֶעָנָן, מִפְּנֵיהֶם, וַיַּעֲמֹד, מֵאַחֲרֵיהֶם.

כ וַיָּבֹא בֵּין מַחֲנֵה מִצְרַיִם, וּבֵין מַחֲנֵה יִשְׂרָאֵל, וַיְהִי הֶעָנָן וְהַחֹשֶׁךְ, וַיָּאֶר אֶת-הַלָּיְלָה; וְלֹא-קָרַב זֶה אֶל-זֶה, כָּל-הַלָּיְלָה.

כא וַיֵּט מֹשֶׁה אֶת-יָדוֹ, עַל-הַיָּם, וַיּוֹלֶךְ יְהוָה אֶת-הַיָּם בְּרוּחַ קָדִים עַזָּה כָּל-הַלַּיְלָה, וַיָּשֶׂם אֶת-הַיָּם לֶחָרָבָה; וַיִּבָּקְעוּ, הַמָּיִם.

The following chart below are all the names extracted from the Exodus verses. Each line is to be read from right to left.

כהת	אכא	ללה	מהש	עלם	סיט	ילי	והו
הקם	הרי	מבה	יזל	ההע	לאו	אלד	הזי
וזהו	מלה	ייי	נלך	פהל	לוו	כלי	לאו
ועיר	לכב	אום	ריי	שאה	ירת	האא	נתה
ייז	רהע	וזעם	אני	מנד	כוק	להוו	יוזו
מייה	עשל	ערי	סאל	ילה	וול	מיכ	ההה
פוי	מבה	נית	ננא	עמם	הועש	דני	והו
מוזי	עזו	יהה	ומב	מצר	הרוז	ייל	נמם
מום	היי	יבמ	ראה	וזו	איע	מנק	דמב

It might seem silly to extract the names like this, but those names are in fact, hidden within the text.

One thing we do know for certain is that the names are powerful. People from all over the world and from all walks of life have used these names to change their lives. I will now extract the names and then go on to give you the powers that each name contains. After that, we will go through 72 EFT/ Meridian tapping sessions , one for each name and tap into this awesome power. We have a lot of work ahead...Let's get to It.

LETTERS ARE PRONOUNCED: Vav Hey Vav

This name is used to get rid of regret in one's life.

LETTERS ARE PRONOUNCED: Yud Lamed Yud

This name is used to recapture a Pure spiritual state

LETTERS ARE PRONOUNCED: Samech Yud Tet

This name is used to create miracles in all areas of life.

LETTERS ARE PRONOUNCED: Ayin Lamed Mem

This name is used to get rid of negative thinking

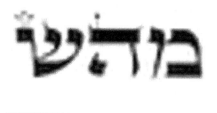

LETTERS ARE PRONOUNCED: Mem Hay Shin

This name is used to bring about deep inner healing

NAME 6

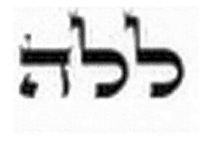

LETTERS ARE PRONOUNCED: Lamed Lamed Hay

This name is used to foster protection during the Dream State and to have prophetic dreams.

LETTERS ARE PRONOUNCED: Alef Kaf Alef

This name is used to create a bridge to reconcile the body, mind and soul.

NAME 8

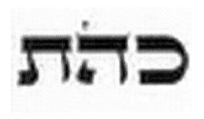

LETTERS ARE PRONOUNCED: Kaf Hay Tav

This name is used to rid yourself and others of stress and negative energy

NAME 9

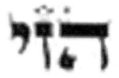

LETTERS ARE PRONOUNCED: Hay Zayin Yud

This name is used to help create a connection to the angelic worlds

LETTERS ARE PRONOUNCED: Alef Lamed Daled

This name is used to protect you from the negative energies of people. Reverses the Evil Eye

LETTERS ARE PRONOUNCED: Lamed Alef Vav

This name is used to reduce the negative influences of an inflated ego.

LETTERS ARE PRONOUNCED: Hay Hay Ayin

This name is used completely transform hatred into love

NAME 13

LETTERS ARE PRONOUNCED: Yud Zayin Lamed

This name is used to foster inner transformation and self sufficiency

LETTERS ARF PRONOUNCED: Mem Bet Hay

This name is used to create peace and to diffuse hostile situations.

NAME 15

LETTERS ARE PRONOUNCED: Hay Resh Yud

This name is used to create a state of mindfulness before you act.

LETTERS ARE PRONOUNCED: Hay Koof Mem

This name is used to create happiness and destroy depression

LETTERS ARE PRONOUNCED: Lamed Alef Vav

This name is used to rid oneself from the Ego.

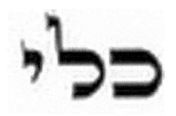

LETTERS ARE PRONOUNCED: Kaf Lamed Yud

This name is used to enhance procreation in mind, body and spirit.

LETTERS ARE PRONOUNCED: Lamed Vav Vav

This name is used to help you be able to hear Gods answers to your prayers.

LETTERS ARE PRONOUNCED: Pey Hay Lamed

This name is used to foster sobriety

LETTERS ARE PRONOUNCED: Noon Lamed Kaf

This name is used to create healing to rid

yourself and the world of sickness

LETTERS ARE PRONOUNCED: Yud Yud Yud

This name is used to create an atmosphere of holiness within your being.

LETTERS ARE PRONOUNCED: Mem Lamed Hay

This name is used to create an open

channel of energy sharing between you

and others.

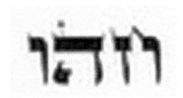

LETTERS ARE PRONOUNCED: Chet Hay Vav

This name is used to free you from the trapping of excessive need for material things.

LETTERS ARE PRONOUNCED: Noon Tav Hay

This name is used to help you find your

voice in all areas of life.

NAME 26

LETTERS ARE PRONOUNCED: Hay Alef Alef

This name is used to create order where there is chaos

LETTERS ARE PRONOUNCED: Yud Resh Tav

This name is used to create generosity in your life. It will help you be able to give freely and purely.

LETTERS ARE PRONOUNCED: Shin Alef Hay

This name is used to create Lasting relationships in your life. More specifically to attract your soulmate.

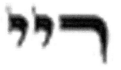

LETTERS ARE PRONOUNCED: Resh Yud Yud

This name is used to purify your heart from hatred and resentment.

LETTERS ARE PRONOUNCED: Alef Vav Mem

This name is used to create bridges between you and other people. bridges between you and spirit so you will be securely connected.

LETTERS ARE PRONOUNCED: Lamed Kaf Bet

This name is used to banish procrastination

LETTERS ARE PRONOUNCED: Vav Shin Resh

This name is used to create positive momentum in your life. If you feel stuck, this is the name you should focus on.

LETTERS ARE PRONOUNCED: Yud Chet Vav

This name is used to locate and remove part your dark nature or shadow body. Once revealed, you can cleanse yourself for a higher purpose.

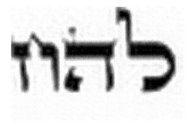

LETTERS ARE PRONOUNCED: Lamed Hay Chet

This name is used to foster humility in your mind and spirit.

LETTERS ARE PRONOUNCED: Kaf Vav Kuf

This name is used to create sexual passion in your life. This passion can also be focused on non-sexual as well.

LETTERS ARE PRONOUNCED: Mem Noon Daled

This name is used to create inner courage and calm

LETTERS ARE PRONOUNCED: Alef Noon Yud

This name is used to help you see the bigger picture when you are hit with obstacles of misfortune.

LETTERS ARE PRONOUNCED: Chet Ayin Mem

This name is used to create a spirit of charity and sharing.

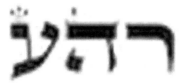

LETTERS ARE PRONOUNCED: Resh Hay Ayin

This name is used to transform your
negative events in life into positive ones.

LETTERS ARE PRONOUNCED: Yud Yud Zayin

This name is used to help you be impeccable with your word.

LETTERS ARE PRONOUNCED: Hay Hay Hay

This name is used to boost self esteem

LETTERS ARE PRONOUNCED: Mem Yud Kaf

This name is used to help you gain spiritual

secrets from the divine realms.

LETTERS ARE PRONOUNCED: Vav Vav Lamed

This name is used to create faith when you feel like you have lost it. It eradicates doubt.

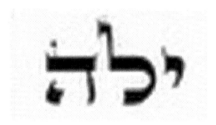

LETTERS ARE PRONOUNCED: Yud Lamed Hey

This name is used to remove the
judgmental side of your personality

NAME 45

LETTERS ARE PRONOUNCED: Samech Alef Lamed

This name is used to create prosperity and
wellbeing in your life.

LETTERS ARE PRONOUNCED: Ayin Resh Yud

This name is used to create a attitude of conviction and faith. You can do anything.

LETTERS ARE PRONOUNCED: Ayin Shin Lamed

This name is used to create world peace,

starting with you.

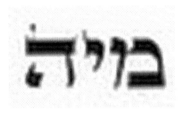

LETTERS ARE PRONOUNCED: Mem Yud Hay

This name is used to create unity and lessen and destroy selfishness.

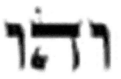

LETTERS ARE PRONOUNCED: Vav Hey Vav

This name is used to help you achieve true happiness.

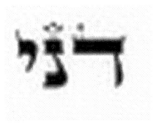

LETTERS ARE PRONOUNCED: Daled Noon Yud

This name is used to help you to foster your worthiness and to reach for what you really want.

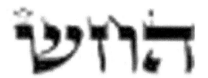

LETTERS ARE PRONOUNCED: Hay Chet Shin

This name is used to destroy guilt

LETTERS ARE PRONOUNCED: Ayin Mem Mem

This name is used to create passion in your life, on all levels.

LETTERS ARE PRONOUNCED: Noon Noon Alef

This name is used to help you become more giving and helpful without having a hidden motive.

LETTERS ARE PRONOUNCED: Noon Yud Tav

This name is used to create a sense of ease and to not fear evil or death. We are spiritual beings and thus do not fear.

NAME 55

LETTERS ARE PRONOUNCED: Mem Bet Hay

This name is used to enhance your

commitment towards a goal.

LETTERS ARE PRONOUNCED: Pey Vav Yud

This name is used to eliminate ego, greed ,

excessive anger and resentment

LETTERS ARE PRONOUNCED: Noon Mem Mem

This name is used to establish connection to your soul so you can find out your true purpose.

LETTERS ARE PRONOUNCED: Hay Resh Chet

This name is used to create spiritual illumination

NAME 60

LETTERS ARE PRONOUNCED: Mem Zadik Resh

This name is used to help you remove the self inflicted prisons you put yourself in mentally.

LETTERS ARE PRONOUNCED: Vav Mem Bet

This name is used to help you purify your body, mind and spirit as well as the earth.

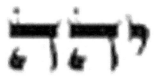

LETTERS ARE PRONOUNCED: Yud Hay Hay

This name is used to help you lead an authentic life and teach others to as well.

LETTERS ARE PRONOUNCED: Ayin Noon Vav

This name is used to create gratitude in your life.

LETTERS ARE PRONOUNCED: Mem Chet Yud

This name is used to help you put your

best foot forward.

LETTERS ARE PRONOUNCED: Daled Mem Bet

This name is used to help you become aware that you are a divine being and that you should act accordingly.

LETTERS ARE PRONOUNCED: Mem Noon Kuf

This name is used to create accountability in your life. You are the creator of your life. This will help you gain control.

LETTERS ARE PRONOUNCED: Alef Yud Ayin

This name is used to create strength in you so you can achieve more and expect good things in life.

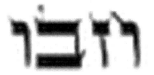

LETTERS ARE PRONOUNCED: Chet Bet Vav

This name is used to help you contact the ones who have departed this world.

LETTERS ARE PRONOUNCED: Resh Alef Hay

This name is used to help you find your direction in all areas of your life. This name will also help to find lost objects.

LETTERS ARE PRONOUNCED: Yud Bet Mem

This name is used to help you recognize the footprints of God when things happen to you. To find the divine lining if you will. Also good to remove financial obstacles.

NAME 71

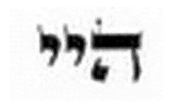

LETTERS ARE PRONOUNCED: Hay Yud Yud

This name is used to help you channel angels, spirits and achieve a state of prophecy.

LETTERS ARE PRONOUNCED: Mem Vav Mem

This name is used to help you completely cleanse your soul.

Chapter 7: Meridian Tapping Using The 72 Holy Names Of God

In this chapter we will put it all together.

The Instructions are fairly similar to my other books on the topic.

1. We do a tapping session on the issue we want to resolve.

2. We will tap using the 72 names and transform those issues . I will provide the images and the letter pronunciations with each tap. All you will do is tap each point while stating the letters of the name. Or, if you feel more comfortable. You can just gaze at the names as you tap each point. That will work too. Tapping 2 to 3 times per point should be sufficient.

NAME 1

LETTERS ARE PRONOUNCED: Vav Hey Vav

This name is used to get rid of regret in one's life.

Tapping Session 1: The Issue

Top of Head: Although I have many regrets in my life, I intend to love and accept myself anyway.

Eyebrow point: I hate having these regrets hold me back

Side of the eye: Will I ever let go of these regrets?

Under eye: I have done many things to be regretful for, but I am willing to let go of them

Under the nose: I need to be free from regret

Chin point: I am a child of God and realize that regrets are a waste of time

Collar bone: I made some mistakes but it is time for me to move on from them

Under Arm Point: We all make mistakes, I am no exception. I will have no regrets

Karate Chop Point: These regrets that I have.

Tapping Session 2: The Holy Name of God

Top of Head: Vav Hey Vav, Vav Hey Vav, Vav Hey Vav

Eyebrow point: Vav Hey Vav, Vav Hey Vav, Vav Hey Vav

Side of the eye: Vav Hey Vav, Vav Hey Vav, Vav Hey Vav

Under eye: Vav Hey Vav, Vav Hey Vav, Vav Hey Vav

Under the nose: Vav Hey Vav, Vav Hey Vav, Vav Hey Vav

Chin point: Vav Hey Vav, Vav Hey Vav, Vav Hey Vav

Collar bone: Vav Hey Vav, Vav Hey Vav, Vav Hey Vav

Under Arm Point: Vav Hey Vav, Vav Hey Vav, Vav Hey Vav

Karate Chop Point: Vav Hey Vav, Vav Hey Vav, Vav Hey Vav

LETTERS ARE PRONOUNCED: Yud Lamed Yud

This name is used to recapture a Pure spiritual state

Tapping Session 1: The Issue

Top of Head: Although I feel spiritually impure, I intend to love myself anyway

Eyebrow point: I yearn to return to state of spiritual purity but I do not know how.

Side of the eye: Will I ever feel that spiritual state I so long for?

Under eye: I will do whatever it takes to feel that connection to spirit

Under the nose: I need to be free from this spiritually impure state that I feel that I have

Chin point: I am a child of God and realize that I am pure spirit

Collar bone: I desire to achieve spiritual peace but can't seem to achieve it

Under Arm Point: We all are one with God, so why don't I feel this?

Karate Chop Point: My Spiritual State

Tapping Session 2: The Holy Name of God

Top of Head: Yud Lamed Yud, Yud Lamed Yud, Yud Lamed Yud

Eyebrow point: Yud Lamed Yud, Yud Lamed Yud, Yud Lamed Yud

Side of the eye: Yud Lamed Yud, Yud Lamed Yud, Yud Lamed Yud

Under eye: Yud Lamed Yud, Yud Lamed Yud, Yud Lamed Yud

Under the nose: Yud Lamed Yud, Yud Lamed Yud, Yud Lamed Yud

Chin point: Yud Lamed Yud, Yud Lamed Yud, Yud Lamed Yud

Collar bone: Yud Lamed Yud, Yud Lamed Yud, Yud Lamed Yud

Under Arm Point: Yud Lamed Yud, Yud Lamed Yud, Yud Lamed Yud

Karate Chop Point: Yud Lamed Yud, Yud Lamed Yud, Yud Lamed Yud

LETTERS ARE PRONOUNCED: Samech Yud Tet

This name is used to create miracles in all areas of life.

Tapping Session 1: The Issue

Top of Head: Although I feel that miracles never happen to me, I intend to love myself and change this.

Eyebrow point: I yearn to return to state where I can create miracles easily

Side of the eye: I know miracles happen, but never to me

Under eye: What do I need to do to create miracles in my life?

Under the nose: I need a miracle in this area of my life

_____

Chin point: I am a child of God and am infused with miraculous powers

Collar bone: Miracles come easily to some, but not for me

Under Arm Point: We all are one with God, so why don't I feel powerful enough to create Miracles?

Karate Chop Point: I intend to be a miracles worker.

Tapping Session 2: The Holy Name of God

Top of Head: Samech Yud Tet, Samech Yud Tet, Samech Yud Tet

Eyebrow point: Samech Yud Tet, Samech Yud Tet, Samech Yud Tet

Side of the eye: Samech Yud Tet, Samech Yud Tet, Samech Yud Tet

Under eye: Samech Yud Tet, Samech Yud Tet, Samech Yud Tet

Under the nose: Samech Yud Tet, Samech Yud Tet, Samech Yud Tet

Chin point: Samech Yud Tet, Samech Yud Tet, Samech Yud Tet

Collar bone: Samech Yud Tet, Samech Yud Tet, Samech Yud Tet

Under Arm Point: Samech Yud Tet, Samech Yud Tet, Samech Yud Tet

Karate Chop Point: Samech Yud Tet, Samech Yud Tet, Samech Yud Tet

This name is used to get rid of negative thinking

LETTERS ARE PRONOUNCED: Ayin Lamed Mem

Tapping Session 1: The Issue

Top of Head: Although I am barraged by negative thoughts, I intend to love myself anyway.

Eyebrow point: I yearn to be free of my negative thoughts

Side of the eye: I know I should think positivity, but it seems impossible

Under eye: What do I need to do to create a more positive mental state?

Under the nose: I need positivity in my life

Chin point: Will I ever be rid of these negative emotional states?

Collar bone: Positive people yield positive changes, I want to be one of them.

Under Arm Point: We all are one with God, so why do I have these negative thoughts?

Karate Chop Point: These negative thoughts that I feel.

Tapping Session 2: The Holy Name of God

Top of Head: Ayin Lamed Mem, Ayin Lamed Mem, Ayin Lamed Mem

Eyebrow point: Ayin Lamed Mem, Ayin Lamed Mem, Ayin Lamed Mem

Side of the eye: Ayin Lamed Mem, Ayin Lamed Mem, Ayin Lamed Mem

Under eye: Ayin Lamed Mem, Ayin Lamed Mem, Ayin Lamed Mem

Under the nose: Ayin Lamed Mem, Ayin Lamed Mem, Ayin Lamed Mem

Chin point: Ayin Lamed Mem, Ayin Lamed Mem, Ayin Lamed Mem

Collar bone: Ayin Lamed Mem, Ayin Lamed Mem, Ayin Lamed Mem

Under Arm Point: Ayin Lamed Mem, Ayin Lamed Mem, Ayin Lamed Mem

Karate Chop Point: Ayin Lamed Mem, Ayin Lamed Mem, Ayin Lamed Mem

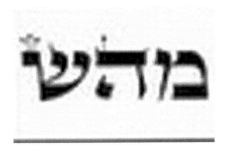

LETTERS ARE PRONOUNCED: Mem Hay Shin

This name is used to bring about deep inner healing

Tapping Session 1: The Issue

Top of Head: I am in need of deep healing but despite that I intend to love who I am right now

Eyebrow point: I yearn to be healed of _____

Side of the eye: I know I can be healed but it seems impossible at the same time

Under eye: What do I need to do to create a healing atmosphere in my life?

Under the nose: I need to be healed NOW

Chin point: Will I ever be healed of _____

Collar bone: healing seems elusive to me, I tried everything.

Under Arm Point: We all are one with God, and so I deserve healing

Karate Chop Point: Healing is coming.

Tapping Session 2: The Holy Name of God

Top of Head: Mem Hay Shin, Mem Hay Shin, Mem Hay Shin

Eyebrow point: Mem Hay Shin, Mem Hay Shin, Mem Hay Shin

Side of the eye: Mem Hay Shin, Mem Hay Shin, Mem Hay Shin

Under eye: Mem Hay Shin, Mem Hay Shin, Mem Hay Shin

Under the nose: Mem Hay Shin, Mem Hay Shin, Mem Hay Shin

Chin point: Mem Hay Shin, Mem Hay Shin, Mem Hay Shin

Collar bone: Mem Hay Shin, Mem Hay Shin, Mem Hay Shin

Under Arm Point: Mem Hay Shin, Mem Hay Shin, Mem Hay Shin

Karate Chop Point: Mem Hay Shin, Mem Hay Shin, Mem Hay Shin

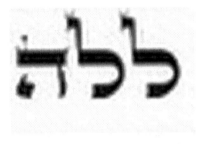

LETTERS ARE PRONOUNCED: Lamed Lamed Hay

This name is used to foster protection during the Dream State and to have prophetic dreams.

Tapping Session 1: The Issue

Top of Head: I have nightmares every night but despite this I can still find love in my heart

Eyebrow point: I yearn to be able to sleep through a night without nightmares

Side of the eye: I know I am protected from harm in my dream state.

Under eye: What do I need to do to create a harmonious dream time?

Under the nose: I desire to have prophetic dreams but I am not sure I can handle them

Chin point: Will I ever be free of negative dream states?

Collar bone: I know I can receive messages in my dreams, but don't know how to receive them

Under Arm Point: We all are one with God, and so I know God speaks through dreams

Karate Chop Point: I dream in peace.

Tapping Session 2: The Holy Name of God

Top of Head: Lamed Lamed Hay, Lamed Lamed Hay, Lamed Lamed Hay

Eyebrow point: Lamed Lamed Hay, Lamed Lamed Hay, Lamed Lamed Hay

Side of the eye: Lamed Lamed Hay, Lamed Lamed Hay, Lamed Lamed Hay

Under eye: Lamed Lamed Hay, Lamed Lamed Hay, Lamed Lamed Hay

Under the nose: Lamed Lamed Hay, Lamed Lamed Hay, Lamed Lamed Hay

Chin point: Lamed Lamed Hay, Lamed Lamed Hay, Lamed Lamed Hay

Collar bone: Lamed Lamed Hay, Lamed Lamed Hay, Lamed Lamed Hay

Under Arm Point: Lamed Lamed Hay, Lamed Lamed Hay, Lamed Lamed Hay

Karate Chop Point: Lamed Lamed Hay, Lamed Lamed Hay, Lamed Lamed Hay

LETTERS ARE PRONOUNCED: Alef Kaf Alef

This name is used to create a bridge to reconcile the body, mind and soul.

Tapping Session 1: The Issue

Top of Head: I feel disconnected from my inner being but I intend to love myself anyway.

Eyebrow point: I yearn to be one in mind, body and spirit

Side of the eye: I know I am one being yet I feel so detached from myself

Under eye: What do I need to do to feel whole?

Under the nose: I desire to have wholeness but can't seem to achieve this state.

Chin point: Will I ever be one in mind, body and spirit?

Collar bone: I know I can receive be a fully integrated being and I will be

Under Arm Point: We all are one with God, and by default we are whole in being.

Karate Chop Point: I am whole and connected

Tapping Session 2: The Holy Name of God

Top of Head: Alef Kaf Alef, Alef Kaf Alef, Alef Kaf Alef

Eyebrow point: Alef Kaf Alef, Alef Kaf Alef, Alef Kaf Alef

Side of the eye: Alef Kaf Alef, Alef Kaf Alef, Alef Kaf Alef

Under eye: Alef Kaf Alef, Alef Kaf Alef, Alef Kaf Alef

Under the nose: Alef Kaf Alef, Alef Kaf Alef, Alef Kaf Alef

Chin point: Alef Kaf Alef, Alef Kaf Alef, Alef Kaf Alef

Collar bone: Alef Kaf Alef, Alef Kaf Alef, Alef Kaf Alef

Under Arm Point: Alef Kaf Alef, Alef Kaf Alef, Alef Kaf Alef

Karate Chop Point: Alef Kaf Alef, Alef Kaf Alef, Alef Kaf Alef

LETTERS ARE PRONOUNCED: Kaf Hay Tav

This name is used to rid yourself and others of stress and negative energy

Tapping Session 1: The Issue

Top of Head: I know I am riddled with stress but i intend to lose myself anyway.

Eyebrow point: I yearn to be stress free

Side of the eye: I know I can be stress free, but how?

Under eye: What do I need to do to be stress free?

Under the nose: I desire to rid myself of negative energy and stress

Chin point: Will I ever be settled and at ease?

Collar bone: I know I can be stress free and will do what it takes to be stress free

Under Arm Point: We all are one with God, and by default I should be stress free but I am not

Karate Chop Point: I intend to be stress free starting now.

Tapping Session 2: The Holy Name of God

Top of Head: Kaf Hay Tav, Kaf Hay Tav, Kaf Hay Tav,

Eyebrow point: Kaf Hay Tav, Kaf Hay Tav, Kaf Hay Tav,

Side of the eye: Kaf Hay Tav, Kaf Hay Tav, Kaf Hay Tav,

Under eye: Kaf Hay Tav, Kaf Hay Tav, Kaf Hay Tav,

Under the nose: Kaf Hay Tav, Kaf Hay Tav, Kaf Hay Tav,

Chin point: Kaf Hay Tav, Kaf Hay Tav, Kaf Hay Tav,

Collar bone: Kaf Hay Tav, Kaf Hay Tav, Kaf Hay Tav,

Under Arm Point: Kaf Hay Tav, Kaf Hay Tav, Kaf Hay Tav,

Karate Chop Point: Kaf Hay Tav, Kaf Hay Tav, Kaf Hay Tav,

LETTERS ARE PRONOUNCED: Hay Zayin Yud

This name is used to help create a connection to the angelic worlds

Tapping Session 1: The Issue

Top of Head: I deeply desire to make contact with angelic being but do not know how

Eyebrow point: Why would angels communicate with me?

Side of the eye: I know I can contact them but don't know how

Under eye: What do I need to do to tap into the angels?

Under the nose: I desire to make deep angelic contacts

Chin point: Will I ever connect to my guardian angel?

Collar bone: I know I can connect with my angel but does it want to connect with me?

Under Arm Point: We all are one with God, and by our nature we can easily connected to angels

Karate Chop Point: I intend to be surrounded by angelic messangers

Tapping Session 2: The Holy Name of God

Top of Head: Hay Zayin Yud, Hay Zayin Yud, Hay Zayin Yud

Eyebrow point: Hay Zayin Yud, Hay Zayin Yud, Hay Zayin Yud

Side of the eye: Hay Zayin Yud, Hay Zayin Yud, Hay Zayin Yud

Under eye: Hay Zayin Yud, Hay Zayin Yud, Hay Zayin Yud

Under the nose: Hay Zayin Yud, Hay Zayin Yud, Hay Zayin Yud

Chin point: Hay Zayin Yud, Hay Zayin Yud, Hay Zayin Yud

Collar bone: Hay Zayin Yud, Hay Zayin Yud, Hay Zayin Yud

Under Arm Point: Hay Zayin Yud, Hay Zayin Yud, Hay Zayin Yud,

Karate Chop Point: Hay Zayin Yud, Hay Zayin Yud, Hay Zayin Yud

LETTERS ARE PRONOUNCED: Alef Lamed Daled

This name is used to protect you from the negative energies of people. Reverses the Evil Eye.

Tapping Session 1: The Issue

Top of Head: I feel like someone has put the evil eye on me but I don't know who it is

Eyebrow point: Why would someone wish bad things on me?

Side of the eye: I know I have a curse on me, but I don't know how to remove it

Under eye: What do I need to do to rid myself of this negative energy?

Under the nose: I desire to rid myself of the negative energy of others.

Chin point: Will I ever be free of the evil eye that has been placed on me?

Collar bone: I know I can get rid of it but I need help

Under Arm Point: We all are one with God, and by our very being, negativity rolls off me.

Karate Chop Point: I intend to be safe from all evil people and the harm they cause.

Tapping Session 2: The Holy Name of God

Top of Head: Alef Lamed Daled, Alef Lamed Daled, Alef Lamed Daled

Eyebrow point: Alef Lamed Daled, Alef Lamed Daled, Alef Lamed Daled

Side of the eye: Alef Lamed Daled, Alef Lamed Daled, Alef Lamed Daled

Under eye: Alef Lamed Daled, Alef Lamed Daled, Alef Lamed Daled

Under the nose: Alef Lamed Daled, Alef Lamed Daled, Alef Lamed Daled

Chin point: Alef Lamed Daled, Alef Lamed Daled, Alef Lamed Daled

Collar bone: Alef Lamed Daled, Alef Lamed Daled, Alef Lamed
Daled

Under Arm Point: Alef Lamed Daled, Alef Lamed Daled, Alef
Lamed Daled

Karate Chop Point: Alef Lamed Daled, Alef Lamed Daled, Alef
Lamed Daled

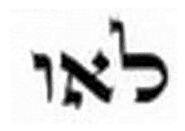

LETTERS ARE PRONOUNCED: Lamed Alef Vav

This name is used to reduce the negative influences of an inflated ego.

Tapping Session 1: The Issue

Top of Head: People tell me that I have an inflated ego, but I intend to love myself anyway

Eyebrow point: Why would I have this ego issue? What happened to me that I would have this?

Side of the eye: I know I am no different than anyone else, why I am I so full of myself?

Under eye: I desire to be more humble in my life but don't think I can

Under the nose: I have been egotistical my entire life, how do I stop it?

Chin point: Will I ever be free of the chains of my ego?

Collar bone: I know I can be free of it

Under Arm Point: We all are one with God, and thus are ego-less

Karate Chop Point: I intend to be humble from now on

Tapping Session 2: The Holy Name of God

Top of Head: Lamed Alef Vav, Lamed Alef Vav, Lamed Alef Vav

Eyebrow point: Lamed Alef Vav, Lamed Alef Vav, Lamed Alef Vav

Side of the eye: Lamed Alef Vav, Lamed Alef Vav, Lamed Alef Vav

Under eye: Lamed Alef Vav, Lamed Alef Vav, Lamed Alef Vav

Under the nose: Lamed Alef Vav, Lamed Alef Vav, Lamed Alef Vav

Chin point: Lamed Alef Vav, Lamed Alef Vav, Lamed Alef Vav

Collar bone: Lamed Alef Vav, Lamed Alef Vav, Lamed Alef Vav

Under Arm Point: Lamed Alef Vav, Lamed Alef Vav, Lamed Alef Vav

Karate Chop Point: Lamed Alef Vav, Lamed Alef Vav, Lamed Alef Vav

LETTERS ARE PRONOUNCED: Hay Hay Ayin

This name is used completely transform hatred into love

Tapping Session 1: The Issue

Top of Head: I Know I harbor hate in my heart, but I intend to love myself anyway

Eyebrow point: Why do I harbor so much hatred in my heart?

Side of the eye: I know I can transform it into love, but don't know how.

Under eye: I desire to be full of love

Under the nose: I have been hateful for most of my life and it is time to turn that into love.

Chin point: Will I ever be free of hatred in my life?

Collar bone: I know I can be free of it and I know I can attract loving energies into my life

Under Arm Point: We all are one with God, and thus are made of love

Karate Chop Point: I intend to be more living, my DNA Is made out of love

Tapping Session 2: The Holy Name of God

Top of Head: Hay Hay Ayin, Hay Hay Ayin, Hay Hay Ayin

Eyebrow point: Hay Hay Ayin, Hay Hay Ayin, Hay Hay Ayin

Side of the eye: Hay Hay Ayin, Hay Hay Ayin, Hay Hay Ayin

Under eye: Hay Hay Ayin, Hay Hay Ayin, Hay Hay Ayin

Under the nose: Hay Hay Ayin, Hay Hay Ayin, Hay Hay Ayin

Chin point: Hay Hay Ayin, Hay Hay Ayin, Hay Hay Ayin

Collar bone: Hay Hay Ayin, Hay Hay Ayin, Hay Hay Ayin

Under Arm Point: Hay Hay Ayin, Hay Hay Ayin, Hay Hay Ayin

Karate Chop Point: Hay Hay Ayin, Hay Hay Ayin, Hay Hay Ayin

LETTERS ARE PRONOUNCED: Yud Zayin Lamed

This name is used to foster inner transformation and self sufficiency

Tapping Session 1: The Issue

Top of Head: I Know I am self sufficient and but feel victimized anyway.

Eyebrow point: I desire so much to be transformed into the person I know I can be

Side of the eye: I know I can transform but feel like I cant.

Under eye: I desire to be all that I can be

Under the nose: I have been a victim my whole life, it's time to take back my strength

Chin point: Will I ever be transformed?

Collar bone: I know I can be free and will be

Under Arm Point: I am self sufficient.

Karate Chop Point: I intend to be me my authentic self

Tapping Session 2: The Holy Name of God

Top of Head: Yud Zayin Lamed, Yud Zayin Lamed, Yud Zayin Lamed

Eyebrow point: Yud Zayin Lamed, Yud Zayin Lamed, Yud Zayin Lamed

Side of the eye: Yud Zayin Lamed, Yud Zayin Lamed, Yud Zayin Lamed

Under eye: Yud Zayin Lamed, Yud Zayin Lamed, Yud Zayin Lamed

Under the nose: Yud Zayin Lamed, Yud Zayin Lamed, Yud Zayin Lamed

Chin point: Yud Zayin Lamed, Yud Zayin Lamed, Yud Zayin Lamed

Collar bone: Yud Zayin Lamed, Yud Zayin Lamed, Yud Zayin Lamed

Under Arm Point: Yud Zayin Lamed, Yud Zayin Lamed, Yud Zayin Lamed

Karate Chop Point: Yud Zayin Lamed, Yud Zayin Lamed, Yud Zayin Lamed

NAME 14

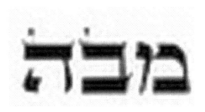

LETTERS ARE PRONOUNCED: Mem Bet Hay

This name is used to create peace and to diffuse hostile situations.

Tapping Session 1: The Issue

Top of Head: I am always surrounded by hostile situations, but intend to love myself anyway

Eyebrow point: I desire to be in peaceful settings but I seem to attract hostility no matter where I go.

Side of the eye: I know I can leave in harmony with everyone around me.

Under eye: I desire the ability to diffuse hostile situations.

Under the nose: Why do I find myself in those situations in the first place?

Chin point: Do I like the drama?

Collar bone: I know I can be free of hostile energies

Under Arm Point: I know I can be free of hostile situations

Karate Chop Point: I AM Peace

Tapping Session 2: The Holy Name of God

Top of Head: Mem Bet Hay, Mem Bet Hay, Mem Bet Hay

Eyebrow point: Mem Bet Hay, Mem Bet Hay, Mem Bet Hay

Side of the eye: Mem Bet Hay, Mem Bet Hay, Mem Bet Hay

Under eye: Mem Bet Hay, Mem Bet Hay, Mem Bet Hay

Under the nose: Mem Bet Hay, Mem Bet Hay, Mem Bet Hay

Chin point: Mem Bet Hay, Mem Bet Hay, Mem Bet Hay

Collar bone: Mem Bet Hay, Mem Bet Hay, Mem Bet Hay

Under Arm Point: Mem Bet Hay, Mem Bet Hay, Mem Bet Hay

Karate Chop Point: Mem Bet Hay, Mem Bet Hay, Mem Bet Hay

LETTERS ARE PRONOUNCED: Hay Resh Yud

This name is used to create a state of mindfulness before you act.

Tapping Session 1: The Issue

Top of Head: I am always acting rashly, but I intend to accept myself anyway.

Eyebrow point: I desire to be more mindful before I act

Side of the eye: I know I can but for some reason I can control myself

Under eye: I need to look at the bigger picture before I act

Under the nose: I need to learn that there is a reason for anything and I need to remain mindful of that.

Chin point: Do I like the drama of being reckless?

Collar bone: I know I can be mindful but don't know how

Under Arm Point: I know I can be mindful before every action but it seems impossible.

Karate Chop Point: I am the embodiment of mindfulness

Tapping Session 2: The Holy Name of God

Top of Head: Hay Resh Yud, Me Hay Resh Yud, Hay Resh Yud

Eyebrow point: Hay Resh Yud, Me Hay Resh Yud, Hay Resh Yud

Side of the eye: Hay Resh Yud, Me Hay Resh Yud, Hay Resh Yud

Under eye: Hay Resh Yud, Me Hay Resh Yud, Hay Resh Yud

Under the nose: Hay Resh Yud, Me Hay Resh Yud, Hay Resh Yud

Chin point: Hay Resh Yud, Me Hay Resh Yud, Hay Resh Yud

Collar bone: Hay Resh Yud, Me Hay Resh Yud, Hay Resh Yud

Under Arm Point: Hay Resh Yud, Me Hay Resh Yud, Hay Resh Yud

Karate Chop Point: Hay Resh Yud, Me Hay Resh Yud, Hay Resh Yud

LETTERS ARE PRONOUNCED: Hay Koof Mem

This name is used to create happiness and destroy depression

Tapping Session 1: The Issue

Top of Head: I am always depressed but I decide today to love myself anyway.

Eyebrow point: I desire to be truly happy but that seems unrealistic

Side of the eye: I know I can be happy but how do I get there?

Under eye: I need to look at the good things in my life

Under the nose: I want to create happiness in my life and I will

Chin point: Do I gain anything from this depression?

Collar bone: I know I can be happy but don't know how

Under Arm Point: I know I can be happy but it seems impossible.

Karate Chop Point: I am the embodiment of happiness, I am going to be happy today

Tapping Session 2: The Holy Name of God

Top of Head: Hay Koof Mem, Hay Koof Mem, Hay Koof Mem

Eyebrow point: Hay Koof Mem, Hay Koof Mem, Hay Koof Mem

Side of the eye: Hay Koof Mem, Hay Koof Mem, Hay Koof Mem

Under eye: Hay Koof Mem, Hay Koof Mem, Hay Koof Mem

Under the nose: Hay Koof Mem, Hay Koof Mem, Hay Koof Mem

Chin point: Hay Koof Mem, Hay Koof Mem, Hay Koof Mem

Collar bone: Hay Koof Mem, Hay Koof Mem, Hay Koof Mem

Under Arm Point: Hay Koof Mem, Hay Koof Mem, Hay Koof Mem

Karate Chop Point: Hay Koof Mem, Hay Koof Mem, Hay Koof Mem

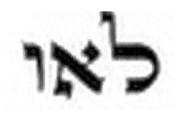

LETTERS ARE PRONOUNCED: Lamed Alef Vav

This name is used to rid oneself from the Ego.

Tapping Session 1: The Issue

Top of Head: I am attached to my ego but I love myself anyway.

Eyebrow point: I desire to free up my ego so I can truly be happy

Side of the eye: I know I can be free of it but don't know how

Under eye: I need to look at the bigger picture and realize my ego is an illusion

Under the nose: I want to create happiness in my life but I can't until I contain the ego

Chin point: Do I gain anything from this ?

Collar bone: I know I can be free of the prison my ego puts me in

Under Arm Point: Ego be gone

Karate Chop Point: I am the embodiment of egolessness

Tapping Session 2: The Holy Name of God

Top of Head: Lamed Alef Vav, Lamed Alef Vav, Lamed Alef Vav

Fyebrow point: Lamed Alef Vav, Lamed Alef Vav, Lamed Alef Vav

Side of the eye: Lamed Alef Vav, Lamed Alef Vav, Lamed Alef Vav

Under eye: Lamed Alef Vav, Lamed Alef Vav, Lamed Alef Vav

Under the nose: Lamed Alef Vav, Lamed Alef Vav, Lamed Alef Vav

Chin point: Lamed Alef Vav, Lamed Alef Vav, Lamed Alef Vav

Collar bone: Lamed Alef Vav, Lamed Alef Vav, Lamed Alef Vav

Under Arm Point: Lamed Alef Vav, Lamed Alef Vav, Lamed Alef Vav

Karate Chop Point: Lamed Alef Vav, Lamed Alef Vav, Lamed Alef Vav

NAME 18

LETTERS ARE PRONOUNCED. Kaf Lamed Yud

This name is used to enhance procreation in mind, body and spirit.

Tapping Session 1: The Issue

Top of Head: I am feeling uncreative and dull but intend to love myself anyway

Eyebrow point: I desire to free up my creativity in mind body and spirit

Side of the eye: I know I can be creative but don't know how

Under eye: I am a creative life force and can bring life into this world in body

Under the nose: I am a creative life force and can bring life into this world in Spirit

Chin point: I am a creative life force and can bring life into this world in Mind

Collar bone: I know I can

Under Arm Point: I am made of God and thus creative by nature.

Karate Chop Point: I am the embodiment of creative energies

Tapping Session 2: The Holy Name of God

Top of Head: Kaf Lamed Vav, Kaf Lamed Vav, Kaf Lamed Vav,

Eyebrow point: Kaf Lamed Vav, Kaf Lamed Vav, Kaf Lamed Vav,

Side of the eye: Kaf Lamed Vav, Kaf Lamed Vav, Kaf Lamed Vav,

Under eye: Kaf Lamed Vav, Kaf Lamed Vav, Kaf Lamed Vav,

Under the nose: Kaf Lamed Vav, Kaf Lamed Vav, Kaf Lamed Vav,

Chin point: Kaf Lamed Vav, Kaf Lamed Vav, Kaf Lamed Vav,

Collar bone: Kaf Lamed Vav, Kaf Lamed Vav, Kaf Lamed Vav,

Under Arm Point: Kaf Lamed Vav, Kaf Lamed Vav, Kaf Lamed Vav,

Karate Chop Point: Kaf Lamed Vav, Kaf Lamed Vav, Kaf Lamed Vav,

LETTERS ARE PRONOUNCED: Lamed Vav Vav

This name is used to help you be able to hear Gods answers to your prayers.

Tapping Session 1: The Issue

Top of Head: I always feel like God doesn't listen to me, but I intend to still feel worthy anyway.

Eyebrow point: Why is God not answering my prayers?

Side of the eye: I know God is listening but don't why God is not answering

Under eye: I am willing to open my spirit so I can hear Gods answers

Under the nose: I am a spark of God and by default God answers all my prayers

Chin point: I am ready to hear God

Collar bone: I know I can hear God

Under Arm Point: I am on with Gods message

Karate Chop Point: I am an open channel to God

Tapping Session 2: The Holy Name of God

Top of Head: Lamed Vav Vav, Lamed Vav Vav, Lamed Vav Vav

Eyebrow point: Lamed Vav Vav, Lamed Vav Vav, Lamed Vav Vav

Side of the eye: Lamed Vav Vav, Lamed Vav Vav, Lamed Vav Vav

Under eye: Lamed Vav Vav, Lamed Vav Vav, Lamed Vav Vav

Under the nose: Lamed Vav Vav, Lamed Vav Vav, Lamed Vav Vav

Chin point: Lamed Vav Vav, Lamed Vav Vav, Lamed Vav Vav

Collar bone: Lamed Vav Vav, Lamed Vav Vav, Lamed Vav Vav

Under Arm Point: Lamed Vav Vav, Lamed Vav Vav, Lamed Vav Vav

Karate Chop Point: Lamed Vav Vav, Lamed Vav Vav, Lamed Vav Vav

NAME 20

LETTERS ARE PRONOUNCED: Pey Hay Lamed

This name is used to foster sobriety

Tapping Session 1: The Issue

Top of Head: I have this addiction to _____ but I still intend to love myself anyway

Eyebrow point: Why so I have this addiction?

Side of the eye: Why Can't I control it?

Under eye: I am willing to let it go but I am afraid

Under the nose: I am a spark of God and will be free of my addiction to _____

Chin point: I am ready for sobriety

Collar bone: I know I can do it

Under Arm Point: I am sober

Karate Chop Point: By the Grace of God

Tapping Session 2: The Holy Name of God

Top of Head: Pey Hay Lamed, Pey Hay Lamed, Pey Hay Lamed.

Eyebrow point: Pey Hay Lamed, Pey Hay Lamed, Pey Hay Lamed.

Side of the eye: Pey Hay Lamed, Pey Hay Lamed, Pey Hay Lamed.

Under eye: Pey Hay Lamed, Pey Hay Lamed, Pey Hay Lamed.

Under the nose: Pey Hay Lamed, Pey Hay Lamed, Pey Hay Lamed.

Chin point: Pey Hay Lamed, Pey Hay Lamed, Pey Hay Lamed.

Collar bone: Pey Hay Lamed, Pey Hay Lamed, Pey Hay Lamed.

Under Arm Point: Pey Hay Lamed, Pey Hay Lamed, Pey Hay Lamed.

Karate Chop Point: Pey Hay Lamed, Pey Hay Lamed, Pey Hay Lamed.

NAME 21

LETTERS ARE PRONOUNCED: Noon Lamed Kaf

This name is used to create healing to rid yourself and the world of sickness

Tapping Session 1: The Issue

Top of Head: I have this illness _____ but chose love instead

Eyebrow point: Why do I have this illness?

Side of the eye: Why can't I heal from it?

Under eye: I am willing to let it go

Under the nose: I am a spark of God and will be free of the illness of _____

Chin point: I am ready for real healing of mind

Collar bone: I am ready for real healing of Body

Under Arm Point: I am ready for real healing of Spirit

Karate Chop Point: By the Grace of God

Tapping Session 2: The Holy Name of God

Top of Head: Noon Lamed Kaf, Noon Lamed Kaf, Noon Lamed Kaf

Eyebrow point: Noon Lamed Kaf, Noon Lamed Kaf, Noon Lamed Kaf

Side of the eye: Noon Lamed Kaf, Noon Lamed Kaf, Noon Lamed Kaf

Under eye: Noon Lamed Kaf, Noon Lamed Kaf, Noon Lamed Kaf

Under the nose: Noon Lamed Kaf, Noon Lamed Kaf, Noon Lamed Kaf

Chin point: Noon Lamed Kaf, Noon Lamed Kaf, Noon Lamed Kaf

Collar bone: Noon Lamed Kaf, Noon Lamed Kaf, Noon Lamed Kaf

Under Arm Point: Noon Lamed Kaf, Noon Lamed Kaf, Noon Lamed Kaf

Karate Chop Point: Noon Lamed Kaf, Noon Lamed Kaf, Noon Lamed Kaf

LETTERS ARE PRONOUNCED: Yud Yud Yud

This name is used to create an atmosphere of holiness within your being.

Tapping Session 1: The Issue

Top of Head: I have this pull towards holiness of being

Eyebrow point: Am I able to achieve holiness?

Side of the eye: Is it presumptuous of me to feel that I can be holy?

Under eye: I am willing to let it go of what I have to be holy

Under the nose: I am a spark of God and by default I am an holiness magnet.

Chin point: I am ready for holiness of mind

Collar bone: I am ready for holiness of Body

Under Arm Point: I am ready for holiness of Spirit

Karate Chop Point: I am holy

Tapping Session 2: The Holy Name of God

Top of Head: Yud Yud Yud, Yud Yud Yud, Yud Yud Yud.

Eyebrow point: Yud Yud Yud, Yud Yud Yud, Yud Yud Yud.

Side of the eye: Yud Yud Yud, Yud Yud Yud, Yud Yud Yud.

Under eye: Yud Yud Yud, Yud Yud Yud, Yud Yud Yud.

Under the nose: Yud Yud Yud, Yud Yud Yud, Yud Yud Yud.

Chin point: Yud Yud Yud, Yud Yud Yud, Yud Yud Yud.

Collar bone: Yud Yud Yud, Yud Yud Yud, Yud Yud Yud.

Under Arm Point: Yud Yud Yud, Yud Yud Yud, Yud Yud Yud.

Karate Chop Point: Yud Yud Yud, Yud Yud Yud, Yud Yud Yud.

LETTERS ARE PRONOUNCED: Mem Lamed Hay

This name is used to create an open channel of energy sharing between you and others.

Tapping Session 1: The Issue

Top of Head: I have this inner desire to be a conduit of energy

Eyebrow point: Am I able to achieve this?

Side of the eye: Am I able to share energy freely?

Under eye: I am willing to let it go of what I have to in order to be an energy conduit?

Under the nose: I am a spark of God and by default a vehicle of energy.

Chin point: I am ready for this

Collar bone: I am ready to be a conduit of energy between people and myself

Under Arm Point: I am ready to be a conduit of energy between people ,myself and spirit

Karate Chop Point: I am energy itself

Tapping Session 2: The Holy Name of God

Top of Head: Mom Lamed Hay, Mem Lamed Hay, Mem Lamed Hay.

Eyebrow point: Mem Lamed Hay, Mem Lamed Hay, Mem Lamed Hay.

Side of the eye: Mem Lamed Hay, Mem Lamed Hay, Mem Lamed Hay.

Under eye: Mem Lamed Hay, Mem Lamed Hay, Mem Lamed Hay.

Under the nose: Mem Lamed Hay, Mem Lamed Hay, Mem Lamed Hay.

Chin point: Mem Lamed Hay, Mem Lamed Hay, Mem Lamed Hay.

Collar bone: Mem Lamed Hay, Mem Lamed Hay, Mem Lamed Hay.

Under Arm Point: Mem Lamed Hay, Mem Lamed Hay, Mem Lamed Hay..

Karate Chop Point: Mem Lamed Hay, Mem Lamed Hay, Mem Lamed Hay.

NAME 24

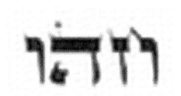

LETTERS ARE PRONOUNCED: Chet Hay Vav

This name is used to free you from the trapping of excessive need for material things.

Tapping Session 1: The Issue

Top of Head: I have a strong desire to acquire material possessions but I love myself anyway

Eyebrow point: Am I able to lessen my desire for material possessions?

Side of the eye: Am I able to let it go?

Under eye: I am willing to let it go but I am afraid of what I will be missing

Under the nose: I am a spark of God and realize that I can't serve God and material possessions equally.

Chin point: I am ready for this

Collar bone: I am ready to lessen my need for material possessions

Under Arm Point: I am ready to be whole and clear

Karate Chop Point: I am divine and desire to acquire heaven rather than material possessions.

Tapping Session 2: The Holy Name of God

Top of Head: Chet Hay Vav, Chet Hay Vav, Chet Hay Vav.

Eyebrow point: Chet Hay Vav, Chet Hay Vav, Chet Hay Vav.

Side of the eye: Chet Hay Vav, Chet Hay Vav, Chet Hay Vav.

Under eye: Chet Hay Vav, Chet Hay Vav, Chet Hay Vav.

Under the nose: Chet Hay Vav, Chet Hay Vav, Chet Hay Vav.

Chin point: Chet Hay Vav, Chet Hay Vav, Chet Hay Vav.

Collar bone: Chet Hay Vav, Chet Hay Vav, Chet Hay Vav.

Under Arm Point: Chet Hay Vav, Chet Hay Vav, Chet Hay Vav.

Karate Chop Point: Chet Hay Vav, Chet Hay Vav, Chet Hay Vav.

NAME 25

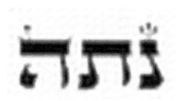

LETTERS ARE PRONOUNCED: Noon Tav Hay

This name is used to help you find your voice in all areas of life.

Tapping Session 1: The Issue

Top of Head: Although I feel stifled, I intend to love myself anyway.

Eyebrow point: I feel like no one hears me.

Side of the eye: I feel like I don't matter and people shouldn't listen to me

Under eye: Why do I feel this way?

Under the nose: I have a right to be heard in this world

Chin point: I am ready to be heard

Collar bone: I am sick and tired of being stifled

Under Arm Point: No one can keep me stifled anymore.

Karate Chop Point: I am divine and I will be heard. I found my voice.

Tapping Session 2: The Holy Name of God

Top of Head: Noon Tav Hay, Noon Tav Hay, Noon Tav Hay.

Eyebrow point: Noon Tav Hay, Noon Tav Hay, Noon Tav Hay.

Side of the eye: Noon Tav Hay, Noon Tav Hay, Noon Tav Hay.

Under eye: Noon Tav Hay, Noon Tav Hay, Noon Tav Hay.

Under the nose: Noon Tav Hay, Noon Tav Hay, Noon Tav Hay.

Chin point: Noon Tav Hay, Noon Tav Hay, Noon Tav Hay.

Collar bone: Noon Tav Hay, Noon Tav Hay, Noon Tav Hay.

Under Arm Point: Noon Tav Hay, Noon Tav Hay, Noon Tav Hay.

Karate Chop Point: Noon Tav Hay, Noon Tav Hay, Noon Tav Hay.

LETTERS ARE PRONOUNCED: Hay Alef Alef

This name is used to create order where there is chaos

Tapping Session 1: The Issue

Top of Head: Although I feel like chaos is all around me, I intend to love myself anyway.

Eyebrow point: I feel like no matter what I do or think it is always chaotic and disordered.

Side of the eye: I feel like I don't have any control over anything in my life.

Under eye: Why do I feel this way?

Under the nose: I intend from now on to attract order into my life.

Chin point: I am ready for stability and order

Collar bone: I am sick and tired of always feeling uncertain

Under Arm Point: Order is coming my way

Karate Chop Point: I am divine and I attract perfect order to the chaos around me

Tapping Session 2: The Holy Name of God

Top of Head: Hay Alef Alef, Hay Alef Alef, Hay Alef Alef.

Eyebrow point: Hay Alef Alef, Hay Alef Alef, Hay Alef Alef.

Side of the eye: Hay Alef Alef, Hay Alef Alef, Hay Alef Alef.

Under eye: Hay Alef Alef, Hay Alef Alef, Hay Alef Alef.

Under the nose: Hay Alef Alef, Hay Alef Alef, Hay Alef Alef.

Chin point: Hay Alef Alef, Hay Alef Alef, Hay Alef Alef.

Collar bone: Hay Alef Alef, Hay Alef Alef, Hay Alef Alef.

Under Arm Point: Hay Alef Alef, Hay Alef Alef, Hay Alef Alef.

Karate Chop Point: Hay Alef Alef, Hay Alef Alef, Hay Alef Alef.

LETTERS ARE PRONOUNCED: Yud Resh Tav

This name is used to create generosity in your life. It will help you be able to give freely and purely.

Tapping Session 1: The Issue

Top of Head: I know I am not the most charitable person in the world but I intend to love myself anyway.

Eyebrow point: I feel like I want to be more giving

Side of the eye: I feel like I don't how to be able to give unconditionally

Under eye: Why do I feel this way?

Under the nose: I intend from now on to give freely of my time

Chin point: I intend from now on to give freely of my money

Collar bone: I intend from now on to give freely of my love

Under Arm Point: I intend from now on to give freely of my spirit

Karate Chop Point: I am divine and I attract generosity of spirit in my life.

Tapping Session 2: The Holy Name of God

Top of Head: Yud Resh Tav, Yud Resh Tav, Yud Resh Tav.

Eyebrow point: Yud Resh Tav, Yud Resh Tav, Yud Resh Tav.

Side of the eye: Yud Resh Tav, Yud Resh Tav, Yud Resh Tav.

Under eye: Yud Resh Tav, Yud Resh Tav, Yud Resh Tav.

Under the nose: Yud Resh Tav, Yud Resh Tav, Yud Resh Tav.

Chin point: Yud Resh Tav, Yud Resh Tav, Yud Resh Tav.

Collar bone: Yud Resh Tav, Yud Resh Tav, Yud Resh Tav.

Under Arm Point: Yud Resh Tav, Yud Resh Tav, Yud Resh Tav.

Karate Chop Point: Yud Resh Tav, Yud Resh Tav, Yud Resh Tav.

NAME 28

LETTERS ARE PRONOUNCED: Shin Alef Hay

This name is used to create Lasting relationships in your life. More specifically to attract your soul mate.

Tapping Session 1: The Issue

Top of Head: Although I am alone right now, I intend to love myself anyway

Eyebrow point: I feel like I want to find my soul mate

Side of the eye: I really want love in my life but don't know if I ever will get it.

Under eye: Do I have a soul mate?

Under the nose: If so, where are they?

Chin point: I feel so alone and I truly want to be with my soul mate

Collar bone: I intend from now on to attract the right person into my life

Under Arm Point: I will resonate love from now on

Karate Chop Point: I know my soul mate is out there and we will find each other.

Tapping Session 2: The Holy Name of God

Top of Head: Shin Alef Hay, Shin Alef Hay, Shin Alef Hay.

Eyebrow point: Shin Alef Hay, Shin Alef Hay, Shin Alef Hay.

Side of the eye: Shin Alef Hay, Shin Alef Hay, Shin Alef Hay.

Under eye: Shin Alef Hay, Shin Alef Hay, Shin Alef Hay.

Under the nose: Shin Alef Hay, Shin Alef Hay, Shin Alef Hay.

Chin point: Shin Alef Hay, Shin Alef Hay, Shin Alef Hay.

Collar bone: Shin Alef Hay, Shin Alef Hay, Shin Alef Hay.

Under Arm Point: Shin Alef Hay, Shin Alef Hay, Shin Alef Hay.

Karate Chop Point: Shin Alef Hay, Shin Alef Hay, Shin Alef Hay.

NAME 29

LETTERS ARE PRONOUNCED: Resh Yud Yud

This name is used to purify your heart from hatred and resentment.

Tapping Session 1: The Issue

Top of Head: Although I am full of resentment, I intend to let it go and love myself

Eyebrow point: I feel like I could explode with resentment

Side of the eye: I really resent _____ and I am having a problem letting it go

Under eye: Can I ever let it go?

Under the nose: I want to let it go of all resentment

Chin point: Resentment no longer serves my life

Collar bone: Resentment has been a poison for me

Under Arm Point: I will let go of it today

Karate Chop Point: I am from the divine, I decide today to let go of my resentment towards _____

Tapping Session 2: The Holy Name of God

Top of Head: Resh Yud Yud, Resh Yud Yud, Resh Yud Yud.

Eyebrow point: Resh Yud Yud, Resh Yud Yud, Resh Yud Yud.

Side of the eye: Resh Yud Yud, Resh Yud Yud, Resh Yud Yud.

Under eye: Resh Yud Yud, Resh Yud Yud, Resh Yud Yud.

Under the nose: Resh Yud Yud, Resh Yud Yud, Resh Yud Yud.

Chin point: Resh Yud Yud, Resh Yud Yud, Resh Yud Yud.

Collar bone: Resh Yud Yud, Resh Yud Yud, Resh Yud Yud.

Under Arm Point: Resh Yud Yud, Resh Yud Yud, Resh Yud Yud.

Karate Chop Point: Resh Yud Yud, Resh Yud Yud, Resh Yud Yud.

LETTERS ARE PRONOUNCED: Alef Vav Mem

This name is used to create bridges between you and other people, bridges between you and spirit so you will be securely connected.

Tapping Session 1: The Issue

Top of Head: I have this inner desire to be a conduit of energy for fellow humans and the divine

Eyebrow point: Am I able to achieve this?

Side of the eye: Am I able to share energy freely between all worlds?

Under eye: I am willing to let it go of what I have to in order to be this bridge between all?

Under the nose: I am a spark of God and by default I can bridge any divide

Chin point: I am ready for this

Collar bone: I am ready to be a conduit of energy between people and myself

Under Arm Point: I am ready to be a conduit of energy between people ,myself and spirit

Karate Chop Point: I am the bridge

Tapping Session 2: The Holy Name of God

Top of Head: Alef Vav Mem, Alef Vav Mem, Alef Vav Mem.

Eyebrow point: Alef Vav Mem, Alef Vav Mem, Alef Vav Mem.

Side of the eye: Alef Vav Mem, Alef Vav Mem, Alef Vav Mem.

Under eye: Alef Vav Mem, Alef Vav Mem, Alef Vav Mem.

Under the nose: Alef Vav Mem, Alef Vav Mem, Alef Vav Mem.

Chin point: Alef Vav Mem, Alef Vav Mem, Alef Vav Mem.

Collar bone: Alef Vav Mem, Alef Vav Mem, Alef Vav Mem.

Under Arm Point: Alef Vav Mem, Alef Vav Mem, Alef Vav Mem.

Karate Chop Point: Alef Vav Mem, Alef Vav Mem, Alef Vav Mem.

LETTERS ARE PRONOUNCED: Lamed Kaf Bet

This name is used to banish procrastination

Tapping Session 1: The Issue

Top of Head: Although I always procrastinate, I intend to love myself anyway

Eyebrow point: Why Do I always procrastinate?

Side of the eye: I can never get anything done.

Under eye: I am willing to let it go of this bad habit today but don't know how.

Under the nose: Procrastination really holds me back

Chin point: I am ready to let it go

Collar bone: I am ready to be a person of action

Under Arm Point: I am ready to do what I have to do to get things done

Karate Chop Point: I am proactive

Tapping Session 2: The Holy Name of God

Top of Head: Lamed Kaf Bet, Lamed Kaf Bet, Lamed Kaf Bet.

Eyebrow point: Lamed Kaf Bet, Lamed Kaf Bet, Lamed Kaf Bet.

Side of the eye: Lamed Kaf Bet, Lamed Kaf Bet, Lamed Kaf Bet.

Under eye: Lamed Kaf Bet, Lamed Kaf Bet, Lamed Kaf Bet.

Under the nose: Lamed Kaf Bet, Lamed Kaf Bet, Lamed Kaf Bet.

Chin point: Lamed Kaf Bet, Lamed Kaf Bet, Lamed Kaf Bet.

Collar bone: Lamed Kaf Bet, Lamed Kaf Bet, Lamed Kaf Bet.

Under Arm Point: Lamed Kaf Bet, Lamed Kaf Bet, Lamed Kaf Bet.

Karate Chop Point: Lamed Kaf Bet, Lamed Kaf Bet, Lamed Kaf Bet.

NAME 32

LETTERS ARE PRONOUNCED: Vav Shin Resh

This name is used to create positive momentum in your life. If you feel stuck, this is the name you should focus on.

Tapping Session 1: The Issue

Top of Head: Although I am stuck in my life, I intend to love myself anyway

Eyebrow point: Why Do I feel so stuck?

Side of the eye: I can never seem to find the momentum I need to move forward.

Under eye: I am willing to let go of this state but don't know how.

Under the nose: Being stuck has held me back for so long

Chin point: I am ready to move forward

Collar bone: I am ready to be a person who thrives

Under Arm Point: I am ready to do what I have to do to get there

Karate Chop Point: I will find my momentum

Tapping Session 2: The Holy Name of God

Top of Head: Vav Shin Resh, Vav Shin Resh, Vav Shin Resh.

Eyebrow point: Vav Shin Resh, Vav Shin Resh, Vav Shin Resh.

Side of the eye: Vav Shin Resh, Vav Shin Resh, Vav Shin Resh.

Under eye: Vav Shin Resh, Vav Shin Resh, Vav Shin Resh.

Under the nose: Vav Shin Resh, Vav Shin Resh, Vav Shin Resh.

Chin point: Vav Shin Resh, Vav Shin Resh, Vav Shin Resh.

Collar bone: Vav Shin Resh, Vav Shin Resh, Vav Shin Resh.

Under Arm Point: Vav Shin Resh, Vav Shin Resh, Vav Shin Resh.

Karate Chop Point: Vav Shin Resh, Vav Shin Resh, Vav Shin Resh.

NAME 33

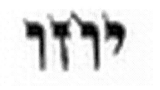

LETTERS ARE PRONOUNCED: Yud Chet Vav

This name is used to locate and remove part your dark nature or shadow body. Once revealed, you can cleanse yourself for a higher purpose.

Tapping Session 1: The Issue

Top of Head: I have dark sides of my that fear but I still intend to love myself anyway

Eyebrow point: I am afraid of the dark recesses of my mind

Side of the eye: I can never seem to escape them

Under eye: I am willing to let go of my shadow and expose it for what it is but I am afraid

Under the nose: I intend to work with my shadow

Chin point: I am ready to transforms the dark sides of my being and make them whole

Collar bone: I am ready to be a person who lives in light not in darkness

Under Arm Point: I am ready to do what I have to do to get there

Karate Chop Point: I will find my light in the darkness of my being

Tapping Session 2: The Holy Name of God

Top of Head: Yud Chet Vav, Yud Chet Vav, Yud Chet Vav.

Eyebrow point: Yud Chet Vav, Yud Chet Vav, Yud Chet Vav.

Side of the eye: Yud Chet Vav, Yud Chet Vav, Yud Chet Vav.

Under eye: Yud Chet Vav, Yud Chet Vav, Yud Chet Vav.

Under the nose: Yud Chet Vav, Yud Chet Vav, Yud Chet Vav.

Chin point: Yud Chet Vav, Yud Chet Vav, Yud Chet Vav.

Collar bone: Yud Chet Vav, Yud Chet Vav, Yud Chet Vav.

Under Arm Point: Yud Chet Vav, Yud Chet Vav, Yud Chet Vav.

Karate Chop Point: Yud Chet Vav, Yud Chet Vav, Yud Chet Vav.

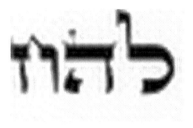

LETTERS ARE PRONOUNCED: Lamed Hay Chet

This name is used to foster humility in your mind and spirit.

Tapping Session 1: The Issue

Top of Head: I know I that I am not exactly full of humility but I intend to love myself anyway

Eyebrow point: I am afraid of humility

Side of the eye: I falsely believe that being humble is being weak

Under eye: I am willing to let go of my ego and allow humility into my life

Under the nose: I intend to work on this side of me

Chin point: I am ready to transform my life and serve humility of spirit

Collar bone: I am ready to be a person who is steeped in humility of spirit

Under Arm Point: I am ready to do what I have to do to get there

Karate Chop Point: Humility is the source of my strength.

Tapping Session 2: The Holy Name of God

Top of Head: Lamed Hay Chet, Lamed Hay Chet, Lamed Hay Chet

Eyebrow point: Lamed Hay Chet, Lamed Hay Chet, Lamed Hay Chet

Side of the eye: Lamed Hay Chet, Lamed Hay Chet, Lamed Hay Chet

Under eye: Lamed Hay Chet, Lamed Hay Chet, Lamed Hay Chet

Under the nose: Lamed Hay Chet, Lamed Hay Chet, Lamed Hay Chet

Chin point: Lamed Hay Chet, Lamed Hay Chet, Lamed Hay Chet

Collar bone: Lamed Hay Chet, Lamed Hay Chet, Lamed Hay Chet

Under Arm Point: Lamed Hay Chet, Lamed Hay Chet, Lamed Hay Chet

Karate Chop Point: Lamed Hay Chet, Lamed Hay Chet, Lamed Hay Chet

LETTERS ARE PRONOUNCED: Kaf Vav Kuf

This name is used to create sexual passion in your life. This passion can also be focused on non-sexual as well.

Tapping Session 1: The Issue

Top of Head: I have sexual issues but I still intend to love myself anyway

Eyebrow point: I am afraid of letting my sexuality flourish

Side of the eye: I falsely believe that sex is bad

Under eye: I am willing to let go of that thought and let my sexually flourish responsibly.

Under the nose: I intend to work on my sexual issues

Chin point: I am ready to transform my sex life

Collar bone: I am ready to be a person who is tapped into my body

Under Arm Point: I am ready to do what I have to do to express my sexuality

Karate Chop Point: Sex is pleasurable

Tapping Session 2: The Holy Name of God

Top of Head: Kaf Vav Kuf, Kaf Vav Kuf, Kaf Vav Kuf.

Eyebrow point: Kaf Vav Kuf, Kaf Vav Kuf, Kaf Vav Kuf.

Side of the eye: Kaf Vav Kuf, Kaf Vav Kuf, Kaf Vav Kuf.

Under eye: Kaf Vav Kuf, Kaf Vav Kuf, Kaf Vav Kuf.

Under the nose: Kaf Vav Kuf, Kaf Vav Kuf, Kaf Vav Kuf.

Chin point: Kaf Vav Kuf, Kaf Vav Kuf, Kaf Vav Kuf.

Collar bone: Kaf Vav Kuf, Kaf Vav Kuf, Kaf Vav Kuf.

Under Arm Point: Kaf Vav Kuf, Kaf Vav Kuf, Kaf Vav Kuf.

Karate Chop Point: Kaf Vav Kuf, Kaf Vav Kuf, Kaf Vav Kuf.

LETTERS ARE PRONOUNCED: Mem Noon Daled

This name is used to create inner courage and calm

Tapping Session 1: The Issue

Top of Head: I feel like I am not able to deal with life but I still intend to find love in myself

Eyebrow point: I am afraid of taking chances

Side of the eye: I falsely believe that being courageous is dangerous

Under eye: I am willing to let go of that thought and allow myself to take more chances in life.

Under the nose: I intend to take more chances and live life with courageous calm.

Chin point: I am ready to grab life by the horns

Collar bone: I am ready to be a person who walks in fearlessness

Under Arm Point: I am ready to do what I have to enhance courage

Karate Chop Point: I am a person of action

Tapping Session 2: The Holy Name of God

Top of Head: Mem Noon Daled, Mem Noon Daled, Mem Noon Daled.

Eyebrow point: Mem Noon Daled, Mem Noon Daled, Mem Noon Daled.

Side of the eye: Mem Noon Daled, Mem Noon Daled, Mem Noon Daled.

Under eye: Mem Noon Daled, Mem Noon Daled, Mem Noon Daled.

Under the nose: Mem Noon Daled, Mem Noon Daled, Mem Noon Daled.

Chin point: Mem Noon Daled, Mem Noon Daled, Mem Noon Daled.

Collar bone: Mem Noon Daled, Mem Noon Daled, Mem Noon Daled.

Under Arm Point: Mem Noon Daled, Mem Noon Daled, Mem Noon Daled.

Karate Chop Point: Mem Noon Daled, Mem Noon Daled, Mem Noon Daled.

LETTERS ARE PRONOUNCED: Alef Noon Yud

This name is used to help you see the bigger picture when you are hit with obstacles of misfortune.

Tapping Session 1: The Issue

Top of Head: I can never see the light at the end of the tunnel but I intend to love myself anyway

Eyebrow point: I am always dumbfounded when bad things happen to me

Side of the eye: I falsely believe that what happens to me has no bigger meaning

Under eye: I am willing to let go of that thought and allow myself to see the bigger picture

Under the nose: I intend to see all hardships as paths in a greater journey

Chin point: I am ready to see the bigger picture

Collar bone: I am ready to be a person who walks in faith

Under Arm Point: I am ready to have a birds eye view of my life

Karate Chop Point: I am a big picture person

Tapping Session 2: The Holy Name of God

Top of Head: Alef Noon Yud, Alef Noon Yud, Alef Noon Yud.

Eyebrow point: Alef Noon Yud, Alef Noon Yud, Alef Noon Yud.

Side of the eye: Alef Noon Yud, Alef Noon Yud, Alef Noon Yud.

Under eye: Alef Noon Yud, Alef Noon Yud, Alef Noon Yud.

Under the nose: Alef Noon Yud, Alef Noon Yud, Alef Noon Yud.

Chin point: Alef Noon Yud, Alef Noon Yud, Alef Noon Yud.

Collar bone: Alef Noon Yud, Alef Noon Yud, Alef Noon Yud.

Under Arm Point: Alef Noon Yud, Alef Noon Yud, Alef Noon Yud.

Karate Chop Point: Alef Noon Yud, Alef Noon Yud, Alef Noon Yud.

LETTERS ARE PRONOUNCED: Chet Ayin Mem

This name is used to create a spirit of charity and sharing.

Tapping Session 1: The Issue

Top of Head: I know I am not the most charitable person in the world but I intend to love myself anyway.

Eyebrow point: I feel like I want to be more giving

Side of the eye: I feel like I don't how to be able to give unconditionally

Under eye: Why do I feel this way?

Under the nose: I intend from now on to give freely of my time

Chin point: I intend from now on to give freely of my money

Collar bone: I intend from now on to give freely of my love

Under Arm Point: I intend from now on to give freely of my spirit

Karate Chop Point: I am divine and I attract generosity of spirit in my life.

Tapping Session 2: The Holy Name of God

Top of Head: Chet Ayin Mem, Chet Ayin Mem, Chet Ayin Mem.

Eyebrow point: Chet Ayin Mem, Chet Ayin Mem, Chet Ayin Mem.

Side of the eye: Chet Ayin Mem, Chet Ayin Mem, Chet Ayin Mem.

Under eye: Chet Ayin Mem, Chet Ayin Mem, Chet Ayin Mem.

Under the nose: Chet Ayin Mem, Chet Ayin Mem, Chet Ayin Mem.

Chin point: Chet Ayin Mem, Chet Ayin Mem, Chet Ayin Mem.

Collar bone: Chet Ayin Mem, Chet Ayin Mem, Chet Ayin Mem.

Under Arm Point: Chet Ayin Mem, Chet Ayin Mem, Chet Ayin Mem.

Karate Chop Point: Chet Ayin Mem, Chet Ayin Mem, Chet Ayin Mem.

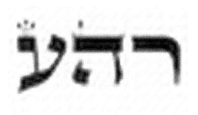

LETTERS ARE PRONOUNCED: Resh Hay Ayin

This name is used to transform your negative events in life into positive ones.

Tapping Session 1: The Issue

Top of Head: I can never seem to turn a negative into a positive in my life but I love myself anyway

Eyebrow point: I am always stuck in negativity and can't seem to change it

Side of the eye: I falsely believe that what happens to me can never been seen in a positive light.

Under eye: I am willing to let go of that thought and allow myself to see the positives in a situation

Under the nose: I intend to see all hardships as opportunity for positivity

Chin point: I am ready to see the positive in my life situations.

Collar bone: I am ready to be a person who walks in faith

Under Arm Point: I am ready to have the ability to turn the negative into the positive.

Karate Chop Point: I am a person of transformation

Tapping Session 2: The Holy Name of God

Top of Head: Resh Hay Ayin, Resh Hay Ayin, Resh Hay Ayin.

Eyebrow point: Resh Hay Ayin, Resh Hay Ayin, Resh Hay Ayin.

Side of the eye: Resh Hay Ayin, Resh Hay Ayin, Resh Hay Ayin.

Under eye: Resh Hay Ayin, Resh Hay Ayin, Resh Hay Ayin.

Under the nose: Resh Hay Ayin, Resh Hay Ayin, Resh Hay Ayin.

Chin point: Resh Hay Ayin, Resh Hay Ayin, Resh Hay Ayin.

Collar bone: Resh Hay Ayin, Resh Hay Ayin, Resh Hay Ayin.

Under Arm Point: Resh Hay Ayin, Resh Hay Ayin, Resh Hay Ayin.

Karate Chop Point: Resh Hay Ayin, Resh Hay Ayin, Resh Hay Ayin.

NAME 40

LETTERS ARE PRONOUNCED: Yud Yud Zayin

This name is used to help you be impeccable with your word.

Tapping Session 1: The Issue

Top of Head: I can never seem to keep my word, but I intend to love myself anyway.

Eyebrow point: I am always reckless with my words

Side of the eye: I am reckless with my words not only to others but to myself as well.

Under eye: I am willing to let go of that but it seems hard for me to do so

Under the nose: I intend to make the effort to be impeccable with my word

Chin point: I am ready to live a life of transparency with my word

Collar bone: I am ready to be a person who walks their talk

Under Arm Point: My word is my bond

Karate Chop Point: I am impeccable with my word

Tapping Session 2: The Holy Name of God

Top of Head: Yud Yud Zayin, Yud Yud Zayin, Yud Yud Zayin.

Eyebrow point: Yud Yud Zayin, Yud Yud Zayin, Yud Yud Zayin.

Side of the eye: Yud Yud Zayin, Yud Yud Zayin, Yud Yud Zayin.

Under eye: Yud Yud Zayin, Yud Yud Zayin, Yud Yud Zayin.

Under the nose: Yud Yud Zayin, Yud Yud Zayin, Yud Yud Zayin.

Chin point: Yud Yud Zayin, Yud Yud Zayin, Yud Yud Zayin.

Collar bone: Yud Yud Zayin, Yud Yud Zayin, Yud Yud Zayin.

Under Arm Point: Yud Yud Zayin, Yud Yud Zayin, Yud Yud Zayin.

Karate Chop Point: Yud Yud Zayin, Yud Yud Zayin, Yud Yud Zayin.

LETTERS ARE PRONOUNCED: Hay Hay Hay

This name is used to boost self esteem

Tapping Session 1: The Issue

Top of Head: I have crushingly low self esteem but I intend to love myself anyway

Eyebrow point: I am always derailed by self esteem issues

Side of the eye: I have zero self esteem and this is ruining my life in so many ways

Under eye: I am willing to let go of that part of me

Under the nose: I intend to increase my self esteem in healthy ways

Chin point: I am ready to live a life of self worth and integrity

Collar bone: I am ready to be the great person that I am

Under Arm Point: I am willing to let myself have high self esteem

Karate Chop Point: I enjoy the person I am and will become

Tapping Session 2: The Holy Name of God

Top of Head: Hay Hay Hay, Hay Hay Hay, Hay Hay Hay.

Eyebrow point: Hay Hay Hay, Hay Hay Hay, Hay Hay Hay.

Side of the eye: Hay Hay Hay, Hay Hay Hay, Hay Hay Hay.

Under eye: Hay Hay Hay, Hay Hay Hay, Hay Hay Hay.

Under the nose: Hay Hay Hay, Hay Hay Hay, Hay Hay Hay.

Chin point: Hay Hay Hay, Hay Hay Hay, Hay Hay Hay.

Collar bone: Hay Hay Hay, Hay Hay Hay, Hay Hay Hay.

Under Arm Point: Hay Hay Hay, Hay Hay Hay, Hay Hay Hay.

Karate Chop Point: Hay Hay Hay, Hay Hay Hay, Hay Hay Hay.

LETTERS ARE PRONOUNCED: Mem Yud Kaf

This name is used to help you gain spiritual secrets from the divine realms.

Tapping Session 1: The Issue

Top of Head: I feel disconnected from the mysteries of the universe

Eyebrow point: I have this strong urge to glean divine secrets but how would I do that?

Side of the eye: I have divine in mind and know I can glean the secrets of the spirit worlds

Under eye: I am willing to let go of that part of me that prevents me from being a messenger of spirit

Under the nose: I am willing to cultivate a daily practice to connected to the divine realms

Chin point: I know I am privy to secrets but am having a hard time hearing them

Collar bone: I am ready to receive

Under Arm Point: I am willing to teach these secrets if divine so wills

Karate Chop Point: I enjoy that deep connection to the divine realms

Tapping Session 2: The Holy Name of God

Top of Head: Mem Yud Kaf, Mem Yud Kaf, Mem Yud Kaf.

Eyebrow point: Mem Yud Kaf, Mem Yud Kaf, Mem Yud Kaf.

Side of the eye: Mem Yud Kaf, Mem Yud Kaf, Mem Yud Kaf.

Under eye: Mem Yud Kaf, Mem Yud Kaf, Mem Yud Kaf.

Under the nose: Mem Yud Kaf, Mem Yud Kaf, Mem Yud Kaf.

Chin point: Mem Yud Kaf, Mem Yud Kaf, Mem Yud Kaf.

Collar bone: Mem Yud Kaf, Mem Yud Kaf, Mem Yud Kaf.

Under Arm Point: Mem Yud Kaf, Mem Yud Kaf, Mem Yud Kaf.

Karate Chop Point: Mem Yud Kaf, Mem Yud Kaf, Mem Yud Kaf.

NAME 43

LETTERS ARE PRONOUNCED: Vav Vav Lamed

This name is used to create faith when you feel like you have lost it. It eradicates doubt.

Tapping Session 1: The Issue

Top of Head: I feel like I have lost my faith but I intend to love myself anyway.

Eyebrow point: I used to believe but now I have grown jaded

Side of the eye: I have more doubt than faith in my life and it is hurting me

Under eye: I am willing to let spirit in again

Under the nose: I am willing to believe again

Chin point: I know I am divine and because of that I have no reason to doubt

Collar bone: I now remember all the times God has provided for me

Under Arm Point: This makes me believe again in gratitude.

Karate Chop Point: I am a person who walks by faith and not by sight.

Tapping Session 2: The Holy Name of God

Top of Head: Vav Vav Lamed, Vav Vav Lamed, Vav Vav Lamed.

Eyebrow point: Vav Vav Lamed, Vav Vav Lamed, Vav Vav Lamed.

Side of the eye: Vav Vav Lamed, Vav Vav Lamed, Vav Vav Lamed.

Under eye: Vav Vav Lamed, Vav Vav Lamed, Vav Vav Lamed.

Under the nose: Vav Vav Lamed, Vav Vav Lamed, Vav Vav Lamed.

Chin point: Vav Vav Lamed, Vav Vav Lamed, Vav Vav Lamed.

Collar bone: Vav Vav Lamed, Vav Vav Lamed, Vav Vav Lamed.

Under Arm Point: Vav Vav Lamed, Vav Vav Lamed, Vav Vav Lamed.

Karate Chop Point: Vav Vav Lamed, Vav Vav Lamed, Vav Vav Lamed.

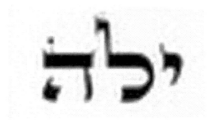

LETTERS ARE PRONOUNCED: Yud Lamed Hey

This name is used to remove the judgmental side of your personality

Tapping Session 1: The Issue

Top of Head: I am a very judgmental person but intend to love myself anyway.

Eyebrow point: I am trying to be less judgmental but I am fining it impossible to do so

Side of the eye: I have more judgment than love in my heart

Under eye: I am willing to let go of my judgmental spirit

Under the nose: I am willing to replace it with more mercy and kindness

Chin point: Who am I to judge anyway?

Collar bone: I am being of love and should only look upon the world with those eyes

Under Arm Point: I now embrace people more

Karate Chop Point: I am a person of mercy

Tapping Session 2: The Holy Name of God

Top of Head: Yud Lamed Hay, Yud Lamed Hay, Yud Lamed Hay.

Eyebrow point: Yud Lamed Hay, Yud Lamed Hay, Yud Lamed Hay.

Side of the eye: Yud Lamed Hay, Yud Lamed Hay, Yud Lamed Hay.

Under eye: Yud Lamed Hay, Yud Lamed Hay, Yud Lamed Hay.

Under the nose: Yud Lamed Hay, Yud Lamed Hay, Yud Lamed Hay.

Chin point: Yud Lamed Hay, Yud Lamed Hay, Yud Lamed Hay.

Collar bone: Yud Lamed Hay, Yud Lamed Hay, Yud Lamed Hay.

Under Arm Point: Yud Lamed Hay, Yud Lamed Hay, Yud Lamed Hay.

Karate Chop Point: Yud Lamed Hay, Yud Lamed Hay, Yud Lamed Hay.

NAME 45

LETTERS ARE PRONOUNCED: Samech Alef Lamed

This name is used to create prosperity and wellbeing in your life.

Tapping Session 1: The Issue

Top of Head: Although I currently lack prosperity, I intend to love myself anyway.

Eyebrow point: I am trying to live in abundance but it seems to be elusive to me

Side of the eye: I have more lack than prosperity in my life

Under eye: I am willing to let go of my spirit of lack

Under the nose: There is literally enough for everyone.

Chin point: Who am I to live in lack?

Collar bone: I am being of God and thus limitless

Under Arm Point: I now embrace prosperity in my life

Karate Chop Point: Prosperity embraces me.

Tapping Session 2: The Holy Name of God

Top of Head: Samech Alef Lamed, Samech Alef Lamed, Samech Alef Lamed.

Eyebrow point: Samech Alef Lamed, Samech Alef Lamed, Samech Alef Lamed.

Side of the eye: Samech Alef Lamed, Samech Alef Lamed, Samech Alef Lamed.

Under eye: Samech Alef Lamed, Samech Alef Lamed, Samech Alef Lamed.

Under the nose: Samech Alef Lamed, Samech Alef Lamed, Samech Alef Lamed.

Chin point: Samech Alef Lamed, Samech Alef Lamed, Samech Alef Lamed.

Collar bone: Samech Alef Lamed, Samech Alef Lamed, Samech Alef Lamed.

Under Arm Point: Samech Alef Lamed, Samech Alef Lamed, Samech Alef Lamed.

Karate Chop Point: Samech Alef Lamed, Samech Alef Lamed, Samech Alef Lamed.

NAME 46

LETTERS ARE PRONOUNCED: Ayin Resh Yud

This name is used to create a attitude of conviction and faith. You can do anything.

Tapping Session 1: The Issue

Top of Head: Although I currently lack strong faith in anything, I intend to love myself anyway

Eyebrow point: I don't seem to have conviction in anything and it really bothers me

Side of the eye: Its like I have lost faith in everything.

Under eye: I need to raise my faith and REALLY believe again.

Under the nose: I need to be strong in my faith

Chin point: Who am I to live without strong faith and

conviction?

Collar bone: I am being of God and thus limitless

Under Arm Point: I now embrace my faith

Karate Chop Point: I can do anything I set my mind upon.

Tapping Session 2: The Holy Name of God

Top of Head: Ayin Resh Yud, Ayin Resh Yud, Ayin Resh Yud.

Eyebrow point: Ayin Resh Yud, Ayin Resh Yud, Ayin Resh Yud.

Side of the eye: Ayin Resh Yud, Ayin Resh Yud, Ayin Resh Yud.

Under eye: Ayin Resh Yud, Ayin Resh Yud, Ayin Resh Yud.

Under the nose: Ayin Resh Yud, Ayin Resh Yud, Ayin Resh Yud.

Chin point: Ayin Resh Yud, Ayin Resh Yud, Ayin Resh Yud.

Collar bone: Ayin Resh Yud, Ayin Resh Yud, Ayin Resh Yud.

Under Arm Point: Ayin Resh Yud, Ayin Resh Yud, Ayin Resh Yud.

Karate Chop Point: Ayin Resh Yud, Ayin Resh Yud, Ayin Resh Yud.

LETTERS ARE PRONOUNCED: Ayin Shin Lamed

This name is used to create world peace, starting with you.

Tapping Session 1: The Issue

Top of Head: Although I am surrounded by turmoil, I intend to love myself anyway

Eyebrow point: I hate knowing that there is so much violence and war in the world

Side of the eye: I wish I could do something about it

Under eye: I can, but I realize that peace first starts within me

Under the nose: I need to find the stillness in peace that is my very being

Chin point: I am full of peace and I radiate it to the entire world

Collar bone: I am being of God and thus full of peace

Under Arm Point: I now embrace a peaceful life and help others do the same

Karate Chop Point: I send peaceful energy to the world

Tapping Session 2: The Holy Name of God

Top of Head: Ayin Shin Lamed, Ayin Shin Lamed, Ayin Shin Lamed.

Eyebrow point: Ayin Shin Lamed, Ayin Shin Lamed, Ayin Shin Lamed.

Side of the eye: Ayin Shin Lamed, Ayin Shin Lamed, Ayin Shin Lamed.

Under eye: Ayin Shin Lamed, Ayin Shin Lamed, Ayin Shin Lamed.

Under the nose: Ayin Shin Lamed, Ayin Shin Lamed, Ayin Shin Lamed.

Chin point: Ayin Shin Lamed, Ayin Shin Lamed, Ayin Shin Lamed.

Collar bone: Ayin Shin Lamed, Ayin Shin Lamed, Ayin Shin Lamed.

Under Arm Point: Ayin Shin Lamed, Ayin Shin Lamed, Ayin Shin Lamed.

Karate Chop Point: Ayin Shin Lamed, Ayin Shin Lamed, Ayin Shin Lamed.

NAME 48

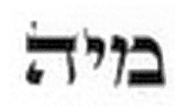

LETTERS ARE PRONOUNCED: Mem Yud Hay

This name is used to create unity and lessen and destroy selfishness.

Tapping Session 1: The Issue

Top of Head: Although I know I am a divisive and selfish person, I intend to love myself anyway

Eyebrow point: I know I have divisiveness and selfishness in my heart and it hurts the people around me

Side of the eye: It also hurts me very much

Under eye: I am willing to learn to be more mindful and cultivate a spirit of unity

Under the nose: I am willing to learn to be more mindful and cultivate a spirit of giving

Chin point: I am full self love and intend to live from that space

Collar bone: I am being of God and thus there is no room for selfishness in my heart

Under Arm Point: I am being of God and thus there is no room for divisiveness in my Soul

Karate Chop Point: I am selfless and whole

Tapping Session 2: The Holy Name of God

Top of Head: Mem Yud Hay, Mem Yud Hay, Mem Yud Hay.

Eyebrow point: Mem Yud Hay, Mem Yud Hay, Mem Yud Hay.

Side of the eye: Mem Yud Hay, Mem Yud Hay, Mem Yud Hay.

Under eye: Mem Yud Hay, Mem Yud Hay, Mem Yud Hay.

Under the nose: Mem Yud Hay, Mem Yud Hay, Mem Yud Hay.

Chin point: Mem Yud Hay, Mem Yud Hay, Mem Yud Hay.

Collar bone: Mem Yud Hay, Mem Yud Hay, Mem Yud Hay.

Under Arm Point: Mem Yud Hay, Mem Yud Hay, Mem Yud Hay.

Karate Chop Point: Mem Yud Hay, Mem Yud Hay, Mem Yud Hay.

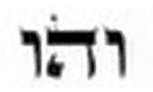

LETTERS ARE PRONOUNCED: Vav Hey Vav

This name is used to help you achieve true happiness.

Tapping Session 1: The Issue

Top of Head: I thought that the material world would bring me happiness but I was wrong

Eyebrow point: I thought that a relationship would bring me happiness but I was wrong

Side of the eye: I thought I knew what happiness was, but I do not, I still feel empty

Under eye: I am willing to learn to what true happiness is

Under the nose: I am willing to learn how to live my life in true happiness that can only come from the spirit

Chin point: I am full divinity and thus true happiness is my natural state

Collar bone: I am being of God and thus all I really know is happiness

Under Arm Point: I am being of God

Karate Chop Point: I am Happiness

Tapping Session 2: The Holy Name of God

Top of Head: Vav Hay Vav, Vav Hay Vav, Vav Hay Vav.

Eyebrow point: Vav Hay Vav, Vav Hay Vav, Vav Hay Vav.

Side of the eye: Vav Hay Vav, Vav Hay Vav, Vav Hay Vav.

Under eye: Vav Hay Vav, Vav Hay Vav, Vav Hay Vav.

Under the nose: Vav Hay Vav, Vav Hay Vav, Vav Hay Vav.

Chin point: Vav Hay Vav, Vav Hay Vav, Vav Hay Vav.

Collar bone: Vav Hay Vav, Vav Hay Vav, Vav Hay Vav.

Under Arm Point: Vav Hay Vav, Vav Hay Vav, Vav Hay Vav.

Karate Chop Point: Vav Hay Vav, Vav Hay Vav, Vav Hay Vav.

LETTERS ARE PRONOUNCED: Daled Noon Yud

This name is used to help you to foster your worthiness and to reach for what you really want.

Tapping Session 1: The Issue

Top of Head: Although I don't feel like I am worth anything in this world, I still accept myself anyway.

Eyebrow point: Why Do I deserve what I want out of life?

Side of the eye: Why Don't I?

Under eye: I really want to increase myself worth but don't know how

Under the nose: I am willing to learn how to love myself more and increase worthiness to go for my dreams

Chin point: I am full divinity and thus full of worth

Collar bone: I am being of God and thus all I am is worthy

Under Arm Point: I am worthy

Karate Chop Point: I know I am

Tapping Session 2: The Holy Name of God

Top of Head: Daled Noon Yud, Daled Noon Yud, Daled Noon Yud.

Eyebrow point: Daled Noon Yud, Daled Noon Yud, Daled Noon Yud.

Side of the eye: Daled Noon Yud, Daled Noon Yud, Daled Noon Yud.

Under eye: Daled Noon Yud, Daled Noon Yud, Daled Noon Yud.

Under the nose: Daled Noon Yud, Daled Noon Yud, Daled Noon Yud.

Chin point: Daled Noon Yud, Daled Noon Yud, Daled Noon Yud.

Collar bone: Daled Noon Yud, Daled Noon Yud, Daled Noon Yud.

Under Arm Point: Daled Noon Yud, Daled Noon Yud, Daled Noon Yud.

Karate Chop Point: Daled Noon Yud, Daled Noon Yud, Daled Noon Yud.

LETTERS ARE PRONOUNCED: Hay Chet Shin

This name is used to destroy guilt

Tapping Session 1: The Issue

Top of Head: Although I am full of guilt, I still intend to love myself anyway

Eyebrow point: Why am I so guilt ridden?

Side of the eye: Will I ever release my guilt about

_____

Under eye: I really want to let it go, it is running my life into the ground

Under the nose: I am willing to learn how to live a life with no guilt

Chin point: I am full divinity and there is no room for guilt in my heart and soul

Collar bone: I am being of God and thus guilt should not exist

Under Arm Point: I am a good person and did the best I could

Karate Chop Point: I release my guilt Now.

Tapping Session 2: The Holy Name of God

Top of Head: Hay Chet Shin, Hay Chet Shin, Hay Chet Shin.

Eyebrow point: Hay Chet Shin, Hay Chet Shin, Hay Chet Shin.

Side of the eye: Hay Chet Shin, Hay Chet Shin, Hay Chet Shin.

Under eye: Hay Chet Shin, Hay Chet Shin, Hay Chet Shin.

Under the nose: Hay Chet Shin, Hay Chet Shin, Hay Chet Shin.

Chin point: Hay Chet Shin, Hay Chet Shin, Hay Chet Shin.

Collar bone: Hay Chet Shin, Hay Chet Shin, Hay Chet Shin.

Under Arm Point: Hay Chet Shin, Hay Chet Shin, Hay Chet Shin.

Karate Chop Point: Hay Chet Shin, Hay Chet Shin, Hay Chet Shin.

LETTERS ARE PRONOUNCED: Ayin Mem Mem

This name is used to create passion in your life, on all levels.

Tapping Session 1: The Issue

Top of Head: I feel like i have lost all passion for life but decide to love myself anyway

Eyebrow point: Why am I so blah about life?

Side of the eye: Will I ever be able to live my life with passion?

Under eye: I really want to finally live my life

Under the nose: I am willing to get rid of these stagnant feeling today

Chin point: I am full divinity and thus a being of passion and purpose

Collar bone: I am being of God and thus my DNA is passion for life

Under Arm Point: I will tap into my passion

Karate Chop Point: I am passion, I am life

Tapping Session 2: The Holy Name of God

Top of Head: Ayin Mem Shin, Ayin Mem Shin, Ayin Mem Shin.

Eyebrow point: Ayin Mem Shin, Ayin Mem Shin, Ayin Mem Shin.

Side of the eye: Ayin Mem Shin, Ayin Mem Shin, Ayin Mem Shin.

Under eye: Ayin Mem Shin, Ayin Mem Shin, Ayin Mem Shin.

Under the nose: Ayin Mem Shin, Ayin Mem Shin, Ayin Mem Shin.

Chin point: Ayin Mem Shin, Ayin Mem Shin, Ayin Mem Shin.

Collar bone: Ayin Mem Shin, Ayin Mem Shin, Ayin Mem Shin.

Under Arm Point: Ayin Mem Shin, Ayin Mem Shin, Ayin Mem Shin.

Karate Chop Point: Ayin Mem Shin, Ayin Mem Shin, Ayin Mem Shin.

NAME 53

LETTERS ARE PRONOUNCED: Noon Noon Alef

This name is used to help you become more giving and helpful without having a hidden motive.

Tapping Session 1: The Issue

Top of Head: I try to be selfless but it seems really hard for me

Eyebrow point: Why am I always giving only to expect it back?

Side of the eye: Will I ever be able to give without a hidden motive?

Under eye: I really want to be selfless and giving

Under the nose: I am willing to get rid of my hidden motives

Chin point: I am full divinity and thus give without expectations

Collar bone: I am being of God and thus my DNA is created without expectation

Under Arm Point: I will tap into my selflessness

Karate Chop Point: I am a giver

Tapping Session 2: The Holy Name of God

Top of Head: Noon Noon Alef, Noon Noon Alef, Noon Noon Alef.

Eyebrow point: Noon Noon Alef, Noon Noon Alef, Noon Noon Alef.

Side of the eye: Noon Noon Alef, Noon Noon Alef, Noon Noon Alef.

Under eye: Noon Noon Alef, Noon Noon Alef, Noon Noon Alef.

Under the nose: Noon Noon Alef, Noon Noon Alef, Noon Noon Alef.

Chin point: Noon Noon Alef, Noon Noon Alef, Noon Noon Alef.

Collar bone: Noon Noon Alef, Noon Noon Alef, Noon Noon Alef.

Under Arm Point: Noon Noon Alef, Noon Noon Alef, Noon Noon Alef.

Karate Chop Point: Noon Noon Alef, Noon Noon Alef, Noon Noon Alef.

NAME 54

LETTERS ARE PRONOUNCED: Noon Yud Tav

This name is used to create a sense of ease and to not fear evil or death. We are spiritual beings and thus do not fear.

Tapping Session 1: The Issue

Top of Head: Although I know I am a spirit of divinity I still fear evil and death

Eyebrow point: Why am I always so fearful despite my divine identity?

Side of the eye: Will I ever be able to live my life without fear of inevitable things?

Under eye: I really want to be fearless in the face of evil

Under the nose: I am willing to get rid of my fear

Chin point: I am full divinity and thus fear doesn't exist

Collar bone: I am being of God and thus fear isn't even in my vocabulary

Under Arm Point: I will tap into my fearlessness

Karate Chop Point: I will not fear death and evil.

Tapping Session 2. The Holy Name of God

Top of Head: Noon Yud Tav, Noon Yud Tav, Noon Yud Tav.

Eyebrow point: Noon Yud Tav, Noon Yud Tav, Noon Yud Tav.

Side of the eye: Noon Yud Tav, Noon Yud Tav, Noon Yud Tav.

Under eye: Noon Yud Tav, Noon Yud Tav, Noon Yud Tav.

Under the nose: Noon Yud Tav, Noon Yud Tav, Noon Yud Tav.

Chin point: Noon Yud Tav, Noon Yud Tav, Noon Yud Tav.

Collar bone: Noon Yud Tav, Noon Yud Tav, Noon Yud Tav.

Under Arm Point: Noon Yud Tav, Noon Yud Tav, Noon Yud Tav.

Karate Chop Point: Noon Yud Tav, Noon Yud Tav, Noon Yud Tav.

NAME 55

LETTERS ARE PRONOUNCED: Mem Bet Hay

This name is used to enhance your commitment towards a goal.

Tapping Session 1: The Issue

Top of Head: Although I have several unfulfilled goals, I intend to treat myself with kindness anyway

Eyebrow point: Why am I always just short of reaching my goals?

Side of the eye: Will I ever be able to truly commit to my goals?

Under eye: I really want to achieve my goals. I know I have it in me

Under the nose: I am willing to commit to my goals right now

Chin point: Me and My Goals are one

Collar bone: I am being of God and thus always fully goal oriented

Under Arm Point: I will tap into commitment

Karate Chop Point: I will achieve my goals

Tapping Session 2: The Holy Name of God

Top of Head: Mem Bet Hay, Mem Bet Hay, Mem Bet Hay.

Eyebrow point. Mem Bet Hay, Mem Bet Hay, Mem Bet Hay.

Side of the eye: Mem Bet Hay, Mem Bet Hay, Mem Bet Hay.

Under eye: Mem Bet Hay, Mem Bet Hay, Mem Bet Hay.

Under the nose: Mem Bet Hay, Mem Bet Hay, Mem Bet Hay.

Chin point: Mem Bet Hay, Mem Bet Hay, Mem Bet Hay.

Collar bone: Mem Bet Hay, Mem Bet Hay, Mem Bet Hay.

Under Arm Point: Mem Bet Hay, Mem Bet Hay, Mem Bet Hay.

Karate Chop Point: Mem Bet Hay, Mem Bet Hay, Mem Bet Hay.

LETTERS ARE PRONOUNCED: Pey Vav Yud

This name is used to eliminate ego, greed, excessive anger and resentment

Tapping Session 1: The Issue

Top of Head: I know I tend to be greedy, but I intend to love myself anyway

Eyebrow point: Why am I so greedy?

Side of the eye: Isn't there enough for everyone?

Under eye: I really want to eliminate that side of me

Under the nose: I am willing to commit to sharing and giving

Chin point: I do know there is enough for everyone including me

Collar bone: I am being of God and greed has no power over me

Under Arm Point: Greed be gone

Karate Chop Point: And it is so

Tapping Session 2: The Holy Name of God

Top of Head: Pey Vav Yud, Pey Vav Yud, Pey Vav Yud.

Eyebrow point: Pey Vav Yud, Pey Vav Yud, Pey Vav Yud.

Side of the eye: Pey Vav Yud, Pey Vav Yud, Pey Vav Yud.

Under eye: Pey Vav Yud, Pey Vav Yud, Pey Vav Yud.

Under the nose: Pey Vav Yud, Pey Vav Yud, Pey Vav Yud.

Chin point: Pey Vav Yud, Pey Vav Yud, Pey Vav Yud.

Collar bone: Pey Vav Yud, Pey Vav Yud, Pey Vav Yud.

Under Arm Point: Pey Vav Yud, Pey Vav Yud, Pey Vav Yud.

Karate Chop Point: Pey Vav Yud, Pey Vav Yud, Pey Vav Yud.

NAME 57

LETTERS ARE PRONOUNCED: Noon Mem Mem

This name is used to establish connection to your soul so you can find out your true purpose.

Tapping Session 1: The Issue

Top of Head: I know I have a true soul purpose, but I have no idea what it is.

Eyebrow point: What is my true purpose in this world?

Side of the eye: Do I even have one?

Under eye: I really want to find it.

Under the nose: I am willing to commit to finding my true soul purpose

Chin point: I do know I have one

Collar bone: I am being of God and by default, I am full of purpose

Under Arm Point: My soul purpose will find me

Karate Chop Point: I have found my soul purpose

Tapping Session 2: The Holy Name of God

Top of Head: Noon Mem Mem, Noon Mem Mem, Noon Mem Mem.

Eyebrow point: Noon Mem Mem, Noon Mem Mem, Noon Mem Mem.

Side of the eye: Noon Mem Mem, Noon Mem Mem, Noon Mem Mem.

Under eye: Noon Mem Mem, Noon Mem Mem, Noon Mem Mem.

Under the nose: Noon Mem Mem, Noon Mem Mem, Noon Mem Mem.

Chin point: Noon Mem Mem, Noon Mem Mem, Noon Mem Mem.

Collar bone: Noon Mem Mem, Noon Mem Mem, Noon Mem Mem.

Under Arm Point: Noon Mem Mem, Noon Mem Mem, Noon Mem Mem.

Karate Chop Point: Noon Mem Mem, Noon Mem Mem, Noon Mem Mem.

NAME 58

LETTERS ARE PRONOUNCED: Yud Yud Lamed

This name is used to help you let go of the past hurts and traumas.

Tapping Session 1: The Issue

Top of Head: Although I am wracked with painful traumas, I decide to love myself anyway

Eyebrow point: I have so many traumas in my life that I can't seem to let go of them

Side of the eye: Do I even have a chance at happiness?

Under eye: I really want to be free of these traumas

Under the nose: I am willing to work through them if I knew how

Chin point: I do know I can

Collar bone: I am being of God and by my nature, I can shed my traumas

Under Arm Point: My traumas will be healed

Karate Chop Point: I am healed of my traumas

Tapping Session 2: The Holy Name of God

Top of Head: Yud Yud Lamed, Yud Yud Lamed, Yud Yud Lamed.

Eyebrow point: Yud Yud Lamed, Yud Yud Lamed, Yud Yud Lamed.

Side of the eye: Yud Yud Lamed, Yud Yud Lamed, Yud Yud Lamed.

Under eye: Yud Yud Lamed, Yud Yud Lamed, Yud Yud Lamed.

Under the nose: Yud Yud Lamed, Yud Yud Lamed, Yud Yud Lamed.

Chin point: Yud Yud Lamed, Yud Yud Lamed, Yud Yud Lamed.

Collar bone: Yud Yud Lamed, Yud Yud Lamed, Yud Yud Lamed.

Under Arm Point: Yud Yud Lamed, Yud Yud Lamed, Yud Yud Lamed.

Karate Chop Point: Yud Yud Lamed, Yud Yud Lamed, Yud Yud Lamed.

LETTERS ARE PRONOUNCED: Hay Resh Chet

This name is used to create spiritual illumination

Tapping Session 1: The Issue

Top of Head: Although I pray and meditate every day, I don't feel like spirit is upon me

Eyebrow point: I crave that special spiritual illumination

Side of the eye: Do I even make the cut?

Under eye: I really want to feel that divine connection and be naturally illuminated

Under the nose: Not for my own sake, but for the sake of the universe

Chin point: I do know I am a divine child

Collar bone: I am being of God and by my nature, I radiate divine illumination

Under Arm Point: My love is strong within me

Karate Chop Point: I am spiritually illuminated

Tapping Session 2: The Holy Name of God

Top of Head: Hay Resh Chet, Hay Resh Chet, Hay Resh Chet.

Eyebrow point: Hay Resh Chet, Hay Resh Chet, Hay Resh Chet.

Side of the eye: Hay Resh Chet, Hay Resh Chet, Hay Resh Chet.

Under eye: Hay Resh Chet, Hay Resh Chet, Hay Resh Chet.

Under the nose: Hay Resh Chet, Hay Resh Chet, Hay Resh Chet.

Chin point: Hay Resh Chet, Hay Resh Chet, Hay Resh Chet.

Collar bone: Hay Resh Chet, Hay Resh Chet, Hay Resh Chet.

Under Arm Point: Hay Resh Chet, Hay Resh Chet, Hay Resh Chet.

Karate Chop Point: Hay Resh Chet, Hay Resh Chet, Hay Resh Chet.

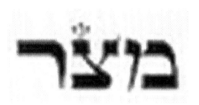

LETTERS ARE PRONOUNCED: Mem Zadik Resh

This name is used to help you remove the self inflicted prisons you put yourself in mentally.

Tapping Session 1: The Issue

Top of Head: Although I am my own worst enemy, I still find it in my heart to love myself

Eyebrow point: I hate the self inflicted prisons I put myself in

Side of the eye: Do I even have a chance at freedom?

Under eye: I really want to feel stable and less mentally destructive

Under the nose: I intend to remove myself imposed roadblocks today

Chin point: I do know I am a divine child and have no reason to be imprisoned by my mind

Collar bone: I am being of God and have no limits

Under Arm Point: So I live in prison?

Karate Chop Point: I am finally free

Tapping Session 2: The Holy Name of God

Top of Head: Mem Zadik Resh, Mem Zadik Resh, Mem Zadik Resh.

Eyebrow point: Mem Zadik Resh, Mem Zadik Resh, Mem Zadik Resh.

Side of the eye: Mem Zadik Resh, Mem Zadik Resh, Mem Zadik Resh.

Under eye: Mem Zadik Resh, Mem Zadik Resh, Mem Zadik Resh.

Under the nose: Mem Zadik Resh, Mem Zadik Resh, Mem Zadik Resh.

Chin point: Mem Zadik Resh, Mem Zadik Resh, Mem Zadik Resh.

Collar bone: Mem Zadik Resh, Mem Zadik Resh, Mem Zadik Resh.

Under Arm Point: Mem Zadik Resh, Mem Zadik Resh, Mem Zadik Resh.

Karate Chop Point: Mem Zadik Resh, Mem Zadik Resh, Mem Zadik Resh.

NAME 61

LETTERS ARE PRONOUNCED: Vav Mem Bet

This name is used to help you purify your body, mind and spirit as well as the earth.

Tapping Session 1: The Issue

Top of Head: My Intention is to become pure of heart, body, mind and soul

Eyebrow point: I intend to purify my thoughts

Side of the eye: I intend to purify my Heart

Under eye: I intend to purify my Mind eye

Under the nose: I intend to purify my Soul

Chin point: I do know I am a divine child and in order to connect I must purify all my senses

Collar bone: I am being of God and I am awash in purity and sanctity

Under Arm Point: I am purity

Karate Chop Point: I am sanctity

Tapping Session 2: The Holy Name of God

Top of Head: Vav Mem Bet, Vav Mem Bet, Vav Mem Bet.

Eyebrow point: Vav Mem Bet, Vav Mem Bet, Vav Mem Bet.

Side of the eye: Vav Mem Bet, Vav Mem Bet, Vav Mem Bet.

Under eye: Vav Mem Bet, Vav Mem Bet, Vav Mem Bet.

Under the nose: Vav Mem Bet, Vav Mem Bet, Vav Mem Bet.

Chin point: Vav Mem Bet, Vav Mem Bet, Vav Mem Bet.

Collar bone: Vav Mem Bet, Vav Mem Bet, Vav Mem Bet.

Under Arm Point: Vav Mem Bet, Vav Mem Bet, Vav Mem Bet.

Karate Chop Point: Vav Mem Bet, Vav Mem Bet, Vav Mem Bet.

NAME 62

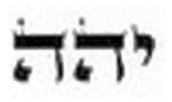

LETTERS ARE PRONOUNCED: Yud Hay Hay

This name is used to help you lead an authentic life and teach others to as well.

Tapping Session 1: The Issue

Top of Head: Although I feel that I am not living authentically, I am choosing to love myself anyway

Eyebrow point: I feel like I am living a lie

Side of the eye: What kind of a role model would I be if I myself can't live authentically?

Under eye: I intend to change that

Under the nose: I intend to live authentically

Chin point: I do know I am a divine child and authenticity is my nature

Collar bone: I am being of God and I am tapping into TRUE authenticity

Under Arm Point: I am Authentic

Karate Chop Point: I am A role model for authenticity

Tapping Session 2: The Holy Name of God

Top of Head: Yud Hay Hay , Yud Hay Hay , Yud Hay Hay.

Eyebrow point: Yud Hay Hay , Yud Hay Hay , Yud Hay Hay.

Side of the eye: Yud Hay Hay , Yud Hay Hay , Yud Hay Hay.

Under eye: Yud Hay Hay , Yud Hay Hay , Yud Hay Hay.

Under the nose: Yud Hay Hay , Yud Hay Hay , Yud Hay Hay.

Chin point: Yud Hay Hay , Yud Hay Hay , Yud Hay Hay.

Collar bone: Yud Hay Hay , Yud Hay Hay , Yud Hay Hay.

Under Arm Point: Yud Hay Hay , Yud Hay Hay , Yud Hay Hay.

Karate Chop Point: Yud Hay Hay , Yud Hay Hay , Yud Hay Hay.

NAME 63

LETTERS ARE PRONOUNCED: Ayin Noon Vav

This name is used to create gratitude in your life.

Tapping Session 1: The Issue

Top of Head: It is hard for me to feel grateful in my life, but I do intend to love myself anyway

Eyebrow point: I feel like an ingrate

Side of the eye: What kind of person am I?

Under eye: I intend to change and feel grateful for everything that I have

Under the nose: I intend to live in a spirit of gratitude

Chin point: I do know I am a divine child and my very soul is gratitude

Collar bone: I am being of God and gratitude is my natural state

Under Arm Point: I am grateful

Karate Chop Point: If the only prayer I ever say is thank you, that will suffice

Tapping Session 2: The Holy Name of God

Top of Head: Ayin Noon Vav , Ayin Noon Vav , Ayin Noon Vav.

Eyebrow point: Ayin Noon Vav , Ayin Noon Vav , Ayin Noon Vav.

Side of the eye: Ayin Noon Vav , Ayin Noon Vav , Ayin Noon Vav.

Under eye: Ayin Noon Vav , Ayin Noon Vav , Ayin Noon Vav.

Under the nose: Ayin Noon Vav , Ayin Noon Vav , Ayin Noon Vav.

Chin point: Ayin Noon Vav , Ayin Noon Vav , Ayin Noon Vav.

Collar bone: Ayin Noon Vav , Ayin Noon Vav , Ayin Noon Vav.

Under Arm Point: Ayin Noon Vav , Ayin Noon Vav , Ayin Noon Vav.

Karate Chop Point: Ayin Noon Vav , Ayin Noon Vav , Ayin Noon Vav.

NAME 64

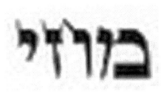

LETTERS ARE PRONOUNCED: Mem Chet Yud

This name is used to help you put your best foot forward.

Tapping Session 1: The Issue

Top of Head: I don't know why I can't make a good impression but I intend to love myself anyway.

Eyebrow point: I feel like I misrepresent myself all the time

Side of the eye: I want to put my best foot forward but I feel afraid

Under eye: I intend to change this about myself

Under the nose: I intend to live with more courage

Chin point: I do know I can make a great impression and I will going forward

Collar bone: I am being of God , it is easy for me to put my best foot forward in all my interactions.

Under Arm Point: I am confident

Karate Chop Point: I am strong

Tapping Session 2: The Holy Name of God

Top of Head: Mem Chet Yud , Mem Chet Yud, Mem Chet Yud.

Eyebrow point: Mem Chet Yud , Mem Chet Yud, Mem Chet Yud.

Side of the eye: Mem Chet Yud , Mem Chet Yud, Mem Chet Yud.

Under eye: Mem Chet Yud , Mem Chet Yud, Mem Chet Yud.

Under the nose: Mem Chet Yud , Mem Chet Yud, Mem Chet Yud.

Chin point: Mem Chet Yud , Mem Chet Yud, Mem Chet Yud.

Collar bone: Mem Chet Yud , Mem Chet Yud, Mem Chet Yud.

Under Arm Point: Mem Chet Yud , Mem Chet Yud, Mem Chet Yud.

Karate Chop Point: Mem Chet Yud , Mem Chet Yud, Mem Chet Yud.

NAME 65

LETTERS ARE PRONOUNCED: Daled Mem Bet

This name is used to help you become aware that you are a divine being and that you should act accordingly.

Tapping Session 1: The Issue

Top of Head: If we are all truly divine, why don't I feel that way?

Eyebrow point: I feel less than divine

Side of the eye: I want to tap into my divine nature but I don't think I have one

Under eye: I intend to change this and shift my attention towards spirit

Under the nose: I intend to live more spiritually so as to feel my divine nature

Chin point: I do know divine is real and therefore I must be a part of that

Collar bone: I am being of God , I am going to start acting like it

Under Arm Point: I am divinity incarnated as myself

Karate Chop Point: All is divine.

Tapping Session 2: The Holy Name of God

Top of Head: Daled Mem Bet, Daled Mem Bet, Daled Mem Bet.

Eyebrow point: Daled Mem Bet, Daled Mem Bet, Daled Mem Bet.

Side of the eye: Daled Mem Bet, Daled Mem Bet, Daled Mem Bet.

Under eye: Daled Mem Bet, Daled Mem Bet, Daled Mem Bet.

Under the nose: Daled Mem Bet, Daled Mem Bet, Daled Mem Bet.

Chin point: Daled Mem Bet, Daled Mem Bet, Daled Mem Bet.

Collar bone: Daled Mem Bet, Daled Mem Bet, Daled Mem Bet.

Under Arm Point: Daled Mem Bet, Daled Mem Bet, Daled Mem Bet.

Karate Chop Point: Daled Mem Bet, Daled Mem Bet, Daled Mem Bet.

LETTERS ARE PRONOUNCED: Mem Noon Kuf

This name is used to create accountability in your life. You are the creator of your life. This will help you gain control.

Tapping Session 1: The Issue

Top of Head: Although I can't seem to take accountability for my life. I intend to love myself anyway.

Eyebrow point: I feel out of control

Side of the eye: I have no accountability and people know it.

Under eye: I need to gain control over my life but I just can't seem to muster the strength

Under the nose: I intend to live with more accountability in my life

Chin point: I do know i create my own reality by stepping up and being accountable

Collar bone: I am being of God , and my very nature is accountability

Under Arm Point: I am accountable

Karate Chop Point: I am in control of my life

Tapping Session 2: The Holy Name of God

Top of Head: Mem Noon Kuf, Mem Noon Kuf, Mem Noon Kuf.

Eyebrow point: Mem Noon Kuf, Mem Noon Kuf, Mem Noon Kuf.

Side of the eye: Mem Noon Kuf, Mem Noon Kuf, Mem Noon Kuf.

Under eye: Mem Noon Kuf, Mem Noon Kuf, Mem Noon Kuf.

Under the nose: Mem Noon Kuf, Mem Noon Kuf, Mem Noon Kuf.

Chin point: Mem Noon Kuf, Mem Noon Kuf, Mem Noon Kuf.

Collar bone: Mem Noon Kuf, Mem Noon Kuf, Mem Noon Kuf.

Under Arm Point: Mem Noon Kuf, Mem Noon Kuf, Mem Noon Kuf.

Karate Chop Point: Mem Noon Kuf, Mem Noon Kuf, Mem Noon Kuf.

NAME 67

LETTERS ARE PRONOUNCED: Alef Yud Ayin

This name is used to create strength in you so you can achieve more and expect good things in life.

Tapping Session 1: The Issue

Top of Head: I have lost my inner strength and expect only bad things in my life

Eyebrow point: I feel like nothing I do will make my life better

Side of the eye: I have no hope and it shows.

Under eye: I need to get strong and start expecting better things for myself

Under the nose: I intend to live with more strength and determination

Chin point: I do expect good things

Collar bone: I am being of God , and all is good

Under Arm Point: I am expecting good things in my life NOW

Karate Chop Point: I have the strength to make good things happen.

Tapping Session 2: The Holy Name of God

Top of Head: Alef Yud Ayin, Alef Yud Ayin, Alef Yud Ayin.

Eyebrow point: Alef Yud Ayin, Alef Yud Ayin, Alef Yud Ayin.

Side of the eye: Alef Yud Ayin, Alef Yud Ayin, Alef Yud Ayin.

Under eye: Alef Yud Ayin, Alef Yud Ayin, Alef Yud Ayin.

Under the nose: Alef Yud Ayin, Alef Yud Ayin, Alef Yud Ayin.

Chin point: Alef Yud Ayin, Alef Yud Ayin, Alef Yud Ayin.

Collar bone: Alef Yud Ayin, Alef Yud Ayin, Alef Yud Ayin.

Under Arm Point: Alef Yud Ayin, Alef Yud Ayin, Alef Yud Ayin.

Karate Chop Point: Alef Yud Ayin, Alef Yud Ayin, Alef Yud Ayin.

NAME 68

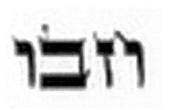

LETTERS ARE PRONOUNCED: Chet Bet Vav

This name is used to help you contact the ones who have departed this world.

Tapping Session 1: The Issue

Top of Head: I deeply desire to make contact with those on the other side

Eyebrow point: Why would the departed communicate with me anyway?

Side of the eye: I know I can contact them but don't know how

Under eye: What do I need to do to tap into the other side?

Under the nose: I desire to make deep contact with the spirit world

Chin point: Will I ever connect and contact _____?

Collar bone: I know I can connect with them but do they want to connect with me?

Under Arm Point: We all are one with God, and by our nature we can easily communicate with all spirits

Karate Chop Point: I intend to be surrounded spiritual connections

Tapping Session 2: The Holy Name of God

Top of Head: Chet Bet Vav, Chet Bet Vav, Chet Bet Vav.

Eyebrow point: Chet Bet Vav, Chet Bet Vav, Chet Bet Vav.

Side of the eye: Chet Bet Vav, Chet Bet Vav, Chet Bet Vav.

Under eye: Chet Bet Vav, Chet Bet Vav, Chet Bet Vav.

Under the nose: Chet Bet Vav, Chet Bet Vav, Chet Bet Vav.

Chin point: Chet Bet Vav, Chet Bet Vav, Chet Bet Vav.

Collar bone: Chet Bet Vav, Chet Bet Vav, Chet Bet Vav.

Under Arm Point: Chet Bet Vav, Chet Bet Vav, Chet Bet Vav.

Karate Chop Point: Chet Bet Vav, Chet Bet Vav, Chet Bet Vav.

LETTERS ARE PRONOUNCED: Resh Alef Hay

This name is used to help you find your direction in all areas of your life. This name will also help to find lost objects.

Tapping Session 1: The Issue

Top of Head: Although I feel like a rudderless ship. I decide today to love myself anyway

Eyebrow point: Why am I so lost?

Side of the eye: I know I need guidance but don't know where to look or who to ask

Under eye: What do I need to do to find some direction?

Under the nose: I desire to finally get on the track I am meant to be on

Chin point: Will I ever find my way?

Collar bone: I intend to find the guidance I need

Under Arm Point: I place my trust in spirit to guide me

Karate Chop Point: I have found my way

Tapping Session 2: The Holy Name of God

Top of Head: Resh Alef Hay, Resh Alef Hay, Resh Alef Hay.

Eyebrow point: Resh Alef Hay, Resh Alef Hay, Resh Alef Hay.

Side of the eye: Resh Alef Hay, Resh Alef Hay, Resh Alef Hay.

Under eye: Resh Alef Hay, Resh Alef Hay, Resh Alef Hay.

Under the nose: Resh Alef Hay, Resh Alef Hay, Resh Alef Hay.

Chin point: Resh Alef Hay, Resh Alef Hay, Resh Alef Hay.

Collar bone: Resh Alef Hay, Resh Alef Hay, Resh Alef Hay.

Under Arm Point: Resh Alef Hay, Resh Alef Hay, Resh Alef Hay.

Karate Chop Point: Resh Alef Hay, Resh Alef Hay, Resh Alef Hay.

LETTERS ARE PRONOUNCED: Yud Bet Mem

This name is used to help you recognize the footprints of God when things happen to you. To find the divine-lining if you will. Also good to remove financial obstacles.

Tapping Session 1: The Issue

Top of Head: If everything that happens has a reason, why can't I see it?

Eyebrow point: Where is the silver lining in my suffering?

Side of the eye: If God does exist why am I not seeing Gods purpose for me in this situation?

Under eye: What do I need to do to find the silver lining?

Under the nose: I desire to finally see for myself that things happen for a reason

Chin point: Will I ever be able to?

Collar bone: I know I need to have faith and that in time I will see the true meaning of things

Under Arm Point: I place my trust in spirit to guide me

Karate Chop Point: I see the divine lining in my life

Tapping Session 2: The Holy Name of God

Top of Head: Yud Bet Mem, Yud Bet Mem, Yud Bet Mem.

Eyebrow point: Yud Bet Mem, Yud Bet Mem, Yud Bet Mem.

Side of the eye: Yud Bet Mem, Yud Bet Mem, Yud Bet Mem.

Under eye: Yud Bet Mem, Yud Bet Mem, Yud Bet Mem.

Under the nose: Yud Bet Mem, Yud Bet Mem, Yud Bet Mem.

Chin point: Yud Bet Mem, Yud Bet Mem, Yud Bet Mem.

Collar bone: Yud Bet Mem, Yud Bet Mem, Yud Bet Mem.

Under Arm Point: Yud Bet Mem, Yud Bet Mem, Yud Bet Mem.

Karate Chop Point: Yud Bet Mem, Yud Bet Mem, Yud Bet Mem.

NAME 71

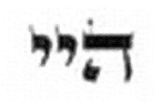

LETTERS ARE PRONOUNCED: Hay Yud Yud

This name is used to help you channel angels, spirits and achieve a state of prophecy.

Tapping Session 1: The Issue

Top of Head: I deeply desire to make contact with spiritual beings and gain insight

Eyebrow point: For some reason I can't seem to make contact

Side of the eye: I know I can contact them but I feel there is a barrier

Under eye: What do I need to do to tap into prophecy of the spirit?

Under the nose: I desire to make deep contact with the spirit world

Chin point: Is it possible to achieve clairvoyance?

Collar bone: I know I can connect with them but do they want to connect with me?

Under Arm Point: We all are one with God, and by our nature we can easily communicate with all spirits.

Karate Chop Point: Prophecy is my birthright and natural state of being

Tapping Session 2: The Holy Name of God

Top of Head: Hay Yud Yud, Hay Yud Yud, Hay Yud Yud.

Eyebrow point: Hay Yud Yud, Hay Yud Yud, Hay Yud Yud.

Side of the eye: Hay Yud Yud, Hay Yud Yud, Hay Yud Yud.

Under eye: Hay Yud Yud, Hay Yud Yud, Hay Yud Yud.

Under the nose: Hay Yud Yud, Hay Yud Yud, Hay Yud Yud.

Chin point: Hay Yud Yud, Hay Yud Yud, Hay Yud Yud.

Collar bone: Hay Yud Yud, Hay Yud Yud, Hay Yud Yud.

Under Arm Point: Hay Yud Yud, Hay Yud Yud, Hay Yud Yud.

Karate Chop Point: Hay Yud Yud, Hay Yud Yud, Hay Yud Yud.

NAME 72

LETTERS ARE PRONOUNCED: Mem Vav Mem

This name is used to help you completely cleanse your soul.

Tapping Session 1: The Issue

Top of Head: Although I feel spiritually impure, I intend to love myself anyway

Eyebrow point: I yearn to return to state of spiritual purity but I do not know how.

Side of the eye: Will I ever feel that spiritual state I so long for?

Under eye: I will do whatever it takes to feel that connection to spirit

Under the nose: I need to be free from this spiritually impure state that I feel that I have

Chin point: I am a child of God and realize that I am pure spirit

Collar bone: I desire to achieve spiritual peace but can't seem to achieve it

Under Arm Point: We all are one with God, so why don't I feel this?

Karate Chop Point: My Spiritual State

Tapping Session 2: The Holy Name of God

Top of Head: Mem Vav Mem, Mem Vav Mem, Mem Vav Mem.

Eyebrow point: Mem Vav Mem, Mem Vav Mem, Mem Vav Mem.

Side of the eye: Mem Vav Mem, Mem Vav Mem, Mem Vav Mem.

Under eye: Mem Vav Mem, Mem Vav Mem, Mem Vav Mem.

Under the nose: Mem Vav Mem, Mem Vav Mem, Mem Vav Mem.

Chin point: Mem Vav Mem, Mem Vav Mem, Mem Vav Mem.

Collar bone: Mem Vav Mem, Mem Vav Mem, Mem Vav Mem.

Under Arm Point: Mem Vav Mem, Mem Vav Mem, Mem Vav Mem.

Karate Chop Point: Mem Vav Mem, Mem Vav Mem, Mem Vav Mem.

Conclusion

Well, there you have it. We have come to the end of our time together. I know it might not seem like a lot but what you have just learned here will unlock your potential in ways that you cant even imagine. Although this book was pretty long, my longest yet. The practices contained are pretty simple. Our connection with source energy is not supposed to be hard. Anyone who tells you that we have to work tirelessly in order to connect to God is , well, misguided in my estiamtlon. **Just using logic alone it doesn't make sense to have to toil to BE what you already ARE.** All it takes is some mindfulness. I am not saying that transformation doesn't require some work, it most certainly does. But the methods to get there do not and are not meant to be complicated. Less is More.

I am confident that by simply gazing at the letters of the 72 names and tapping while doing so you will gain great benefit. They are, after all, the 72 names of God.

Disclaimer

The Information in this book is for educational purposes only and not for treatment, diagnosis or prescription of any diseases or life situations. All advice is for educational purposes only. The Author and the publisher of this book are in no way liable for any misuse of the material. In addition, you agree to purchase this book as is. I Cannot Promise you results.

About The Author

Doron Alon is a bestselling author of 50 books, in 6 different genres and is founder of Numinosity Press Inc.

Before he became an author and teacher, Doron majored in Business and Psychology, spending several years as an Entrepreneur, Wall Street Consultant and Healthcare Analyst. During that whole time, he pursued his intellectual and spiritual passions, leading him to the life that he leads today... One of teaching and service.

Now he writes on a wide variety of topics including History, Self-help, Self-Publishing, Spirituality and health related topics. Doron's background and 24 years of experience in meditation training, Meridian tapping (also known as E.F.T), Subliminal Messaging and other modalities has made him a much sought after expert in the self help and spirituality fields. He is also a up-and-coming expert in the self publishing field and health related topics. His conversational writing style and his ability to take complex topics and make them easily accessible has gained him popularity in the genres that he writes for. As he says " Translating esoteric topics and making them easy to understand" is his area of expertise.

Made in the USA
Middletown, DE
28 September 2019